# London
## The story of a city

Fay Ross-Magenty

Macdonald

**Editorial research and design** Sarah Tyzack
**Reference section** Angela Murphy
**Picture Research** Jenny de Gex and Jenny Golden
**Production** Rosemary Bishop

First published 1979

Macdonald Educational Ltd
Holywell House
Worship Street
London EC2A 2EN

© Macdonald Educational 1979

ISBN 0 356 06308 9

Made and printed by
Morrison & Gibb Limited
Edinburgh, Scotland

The Author would like to thank The Museum of
London, the G.L.C., the Port of London Authority,
the many people in the City and all those who have
kindly provided information and advice.

# Contents

# London's people

One of the first things a visitor to London will be aware of is the number and variety of people in the city. This is especially noticeable in the morning and evening "rush hours", when over a million people are going to or from work in central London. The streets are jammed with traffic and crowds hurry in a great tide of humanity along the pavements. Some are Londoners who have lived in London all their lives, some are working in London for a short time. Many are "commuters" who prefer to live outside London and travel in daily. People also come on short visits. Some come just for the day and others are foreign tourists.

So London is not only full of Londoners, but of people from all over the country and from every part of the world. They are all there for different reasons, leading their own lives. Each person has their own particular idea of "London" and what it means to them.

People are as much part of a city as its buildings. It is people that, over the centuries, have made the London that we have today.

◄ Crowds of commuters hurrying across London Bridge in the morning "rush-hour". They are some of the 44,000 people who arrive at London Bridge Station every morning from places in south-east England. Many commuters have to leave home before 7 a.m. and do not get home till late in the evening.

▲ Shopping for the latest fashions in King's Road, Chelsea. Many young people come to live and work in London for a few years after leaving school or college.

◄ A street stall doing a roaring trade in jellied eels, prawns and shellfish like cockles, mussels and whelks. For centuries oysters were very cheap and they too were sold in the London streets. Now they are an expensive delicacy sold in smart restaurants.

◄ Shoppers wait for buses outside a big store in Oxford Street. Many people come to London just for the day. They can shop, go sightseeing, visit an exhibition or go to the theatre or a concert.

▼ To many people London means home. For this little boy, London is the street where he lives, the small shops nearby and the park where he plays. He may never have been to the centre of the city.

◄ Every February the Chinese community in London celebrates the Chinese New Year with music and dancing. People of many nationalities come to live and work in London. They often preserve the traditions and customs of their own country.

▼ People from all over the world visit London either as tourists or for a special reason. Here, an Arab gentleman is going to Harley Street. He may be going to see one of the medical specialists for which Harley Street is famous.

# City of contrasts

London is a vast city with so many different kinds of places and buildings that it is difficult to sort out one part from another or to see how they all fit together. It is rather like a giant jigsaw puzzle.

Famous buildings, offices, banks, department stores, specialist shops, markets, high-rise blocks, elegant squares, concert halls, parks, are all part of London. Different areas of the city often have their own special character. Knightsbridge and Mayfair are "smart" areas; Oxford Street and Regent Street are famous for their shops. Shaftesbury Avenue is full of theatres and Fleet Street is the centre of the newspaper world. Changes between each area can be very sudden and exploring London can be like stepping from one piece of the jigsaw to the next. It takes a long time and a lot of rides on the top of buses to fit all the pieces together.

London is like a puzzle because it seems to have no plan. It is a city that has grown as if it had a life of its own. One way to understand why it has grown up in this way is to look back into the city's past.

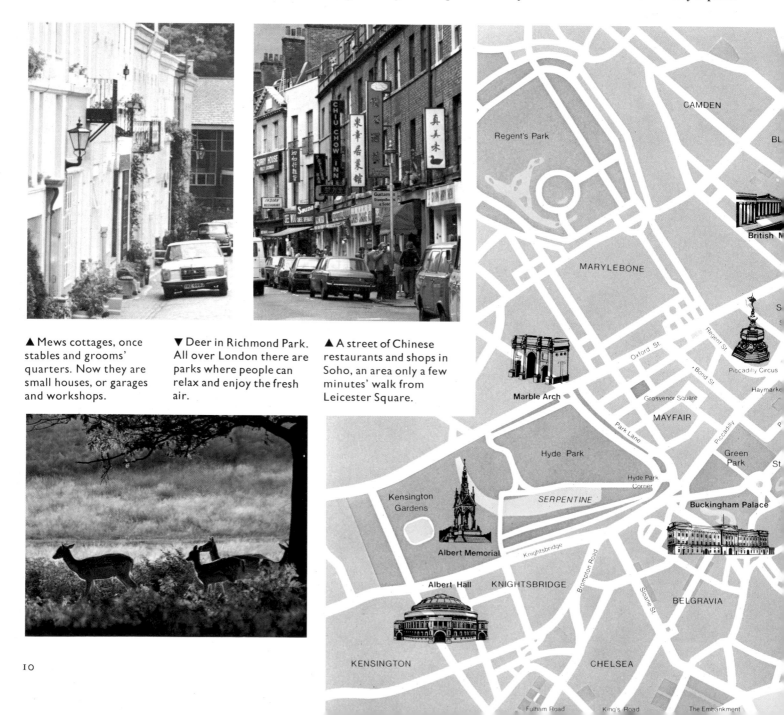

▲ Mews cottages, once stables and grooms' quarters. Now they are small houses, or garages and workshops.

▼ Deer in Richmond Park. All over London there are parks where people can relax and enjoy the fresh air.

▲ A street of Chinese restaurants and shops in Soho, an area only a few minutes' walk from Leicester Square.

▶ Houses and shops overlooking a green. As London spread, places that were once villages in the country were absorbed and became part of Greater London. They have often kept their village atmosphere and are pleasant places to live.

◀ The bright lights and large cinemas of Leicester Square in London's West End. This is where many of the important film premieres take place.

▼ The maps show Central London in detail and the large area known as Greater London.

▲ A street in the City, the business centre of London. Inside imposing buildings and massive office blocks, international deals involving many millions of pounds take place.

▼ Along the river and in East London's dockland many old warehouses are to let or lie empty awaiting redevelopment plans.

HOLBORN

THE CITY

Bishopsgate

Petticoat Lane

Newgate St

Cheapside

Threadneedle St.

Lombard St.

King William St.

St. Paul's Cathedral

Fleet St.

The Monument

Tower of London

Queen Victoria St.

COVENT GARDEN

Strand

RIVER THAMES

London Bridge

Tower Bridge

Trafalgar Square

SOUTHWARK

Downing St.

Whitehall

Westminster Bridge

Greater London

Parliament Square

LAMBETH

Big Ben

WESTMINSTER

VAUXHALL

BATTERSEA

# Londinium

London began nearly 2000 years ago as a Roman town. It grew up at one end of the bridge that the Romans built across the Thames when they invaded Britain. Ships bringing supplies for the army sailed right up the Thames and unloaded near the bridge. Roads were built linking the settlement with the rest of the country and it soon became a flourishing trading town.

The Romans named the town *Londinium*. By 100 A.D. it was the capital of the Roman province of Britain and had fine public buildings of brick and stone. The officials appointed by the Emperor had their headquarters there.

About 200 A.D. a massive wall was built around the city. The Roman Empire gradually broke up and by 410 A.D. the Roman army had left Britain and the city lost its importance. Many people left and its buildings became ruins. In the centuries that followed, Saxons and Danes invaded Britain. Over the years, London's trade recovered and by Norman times it was once again a prosperous city.

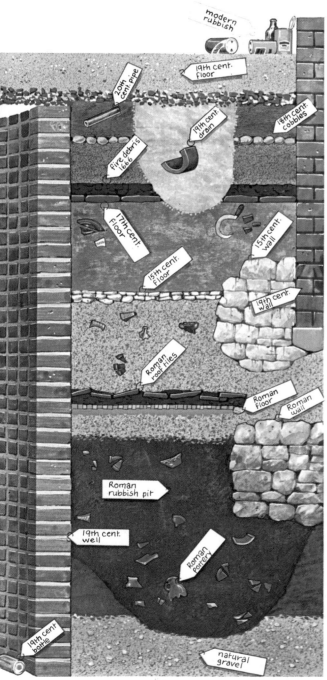

modern rubbish
19th cent. floor
20th cent. pipe
19th cent. drain
18th cent. cobbles
fire debris 1666
17th cent. floor
15th cent. wall
15th cent. floor
19th cent. wall
Roman roof tiles
Roman floor
Roman wall
Roman rubbish pit
19th cent. well
Roman pottery
19th cent. bottle
natural gravel

▲ A museum display of a Roman Londoner's kitchen. All the pottery, glass, and metal cooking pots have been excavated in London. The large, pointed jars contained fish sauce, which was imported from Spain. Wine and olive oil were also imported from the Mediterranean.

◄ A diagram showing what might lie under the cellar of a Victorian office block in the City. It shows how early layers may be broken by later building. Archaeologists date the various layers by studying the objects they find in them.

## Under the City

People have been living in the part of London known as "the City" for nearly two thousand years. Stones, bricks and other building materials have been brought into the city for generations. Until recently, they have never been taken away again when old buildings were demolished, so the level of the ground has gradually risen. Roman London now lies four to six metres below modern street level and under the cellars of many offices, shops and banks.

When sites are cleared for redevelopment, archaeologists are now allowed to excavate the site before the mechanical diggers and pile-driving equipment move in. This is because the foundations of modern tower blocks have to be dug so deep that valuable evidence about London's past is destroyed for ever.

▲ *Londinium* in about 200 A.D., soon after the building of the wall. Gates led out through the wall which was 2.5m thick and probably 6m high. The block of buildings where the city wall bends inwards is the fort. In the centre of the city is the *basilica* (town hall) and open *forum* surrounded by a colonnade of shops.

The city wall of medieval London was built on the foundations of the Roman wall and London did not extend much beyond it until the 16th century. Today, the business centre of London, still known as the "square mile" or "the City", stands on this site.

▶ This gravestone of a Roman soldier was found in London. He carries wax tablets to write on, so he may have had a clerical job on the Governor's staff. Soldiers stationed in *Londinium* also performed guard and ceremonial duties.

## Roman Londoners

*Londinium* was a lively city whose inhabitants came from all over the Roman Empire. They brought with them the Roman way of life. The houses they built, their furniture, food and way of dressing were Roman and their common language was Latin.

Every day the forum was crowded with people from all walks of life: officials on their way to the *basilica*, soldiers from the fort, businessmen talking in groups, women and children, slaves on errands and people shopping. Women wore long tunics and had elaborate hairstyles held in place with decorated hairpins. Men usually wore short tunics. Long white togas got dirty in the muddy streets and were only used on formal occasions. In cold weather people wore thick British-made cloaks.

Along the streets, traders and craftsmen such as carpenters, blacksmiths, goldsmiths and cutlers had their workshops. There were temples and statues and near the river was a public bath house with hot and warm rooms and underfloor heating.

Down at the quays, ships from abroad unloaded goods that would sell well in the shops: glossy red pottery, glass, little statuettes, olive oil, wine and the fish sauce that was essential in Roman cookery. They also brought messages and news, keeping people up to date with the latest events in the Empire.

# The medieval city

Medieval London was a busy and thriving city. The wooden bridge was replaced with one of stone and the Saxon church of St Paul's was re-built and greatly extended. There were also many other beautiful churches and some fine stone houses belonging to rich merchants and noblemen. In the timber-framed houses that overhung the narrow streets were the homes and workshops of many traders and craftsmen, such as goldsmiths, armourers, saddlers, tailors and leather and metal workers.

London became the capital of England in medieval times. At Westminster, about two miles up river from the medieval city, stood a great abbey and a royal palace. Originally the king and his court travelled around the country seeing to affairs of state; but as governing the country became more complicated, it was more practical to base the government at Westminster which was the king's main residence. Law courts were also established there and Westminster became the meeting place for Parliament.

Spectacle makers          Vintners

## The guilds

A guild was originally a group of people with a common interest who met together to worship and to help one another. In London there were four Bridge guilds which helped with the upkeep of the bridge, a Pilgrims' guild, and many craft and trade guilds. The craft and trade guilds also supervised the training of apprentices, controlled standards and prices and tried to prevent outsiders from setting up in competition with their members.

There were fewer trade guilds than craft guilds. Their members were successful business-men dealing in overseas trade. The trade guilds, such as the Mercers, the Grocers, the Drapers and the Vintners, were rich and they were the first guilds to buy royal charters and become "companies" with special rights and powers. By the end of the 14th century the leading companies were so powerful that they elected all the important members of the city's government. They built large halls in which to meet and on special occasions wore robes called "liveries". London still has livery companies. Some of the old ones, like the Long-bowstring Makers, have faded out, but new ones, such as the Guild of Air Pilots and Air Navigators, have come into being. The guilds support charities and education and some still control apprenticeship and standards.

▶ Two young men, who have served their seven year apprenticeships with a master craftsman, are showing off their skills to the head of the guild. If he is satisfied with their work they will be able to become members.

▲ Many street names in the City date from medieval times when certain trades concentrated in one street.

▼ The Lord Mayor's procession is held once a year when the new Lord Mayor is sworn in. London's first Mayor was elected in 1191. In the City he is second only to the sovereign.

14

## Sports and festivities

According to one writer, medieval London was a very cheerful city. Saints' days and religious festivals were holidays, and there was feasting and dancing. At Lent, boys played at mock battles and the sons of noblemen rode out on their horses to practise the arts of war.

Sometimes there was horse-racing near the cattle market at Smithfield. Bear-baiting was very popular and drew excited crowds. In the fields outside the city, people played football or practised archery or wrestling. In winter the marshy ground froze over and boys slid wildly about on the ice wearing bone skates.

On special royal occasions there were splendid processions through the decorated streets. When tournaments became fashionable, they were sometimes held in Cheapside, the wide main street and were very popular.

▼ A baker who has sold impure or underweight loaves being dragged through the streets on a wooden sledge. A loaf is tied around his neck so everyone can see what he has done. Butchers who sold rotten meat were put in the public pillory.

▲ The earliest known view of London, seen from the Tower where a prisoner is being ransomed. In the distance is London Bridge. The bridge is lined with houses and shops: on the left is the chapel of St Thomas Becket. Beyond the bridge rise the roofs and spires of the city.

▼ Pilgrims on their way to Canterbury to worship at the shrine of St Thomas Becket, London's saint. Pilgrims met in groups at St Thomas's chapel on London Bridge. The journey took five days. They came back with badges in their hats and flasks of holy water.

## A city of churches

The Church was very important in medieval London and the city's skyline was a mass of church spires and towers. Londoners worshipped regularly in their own parish churches and placed great importance on elaborate funerals and prayers for the souls of the dead.

There were also a great many monasteries in and around the city. Religious orders ran hospitals and schools and cared for the old and the poor, for there was no welfare state.

St Paul's was the city's main church and place of worship and its huge nave was also the city's main meeting place. Lawyers and public letter-writers could be found there, businessmen met there and people strolled up and down chatting to their friends. In 1385, young people were banned from playing ball games in the church because windows had been broken.

**London about 1560**
By this time building had spread beyond the city wall which
was built on Roman foundations. But open fields were still
within ten or fifteen minutes' walk of the centre of the city.
On the left of the map is Westminster. A wide road leads from
the Abbey through the rambling palace of Whitehall to Charing
Cross. From there the road curves along the Strand which was
lined with splendid houses.

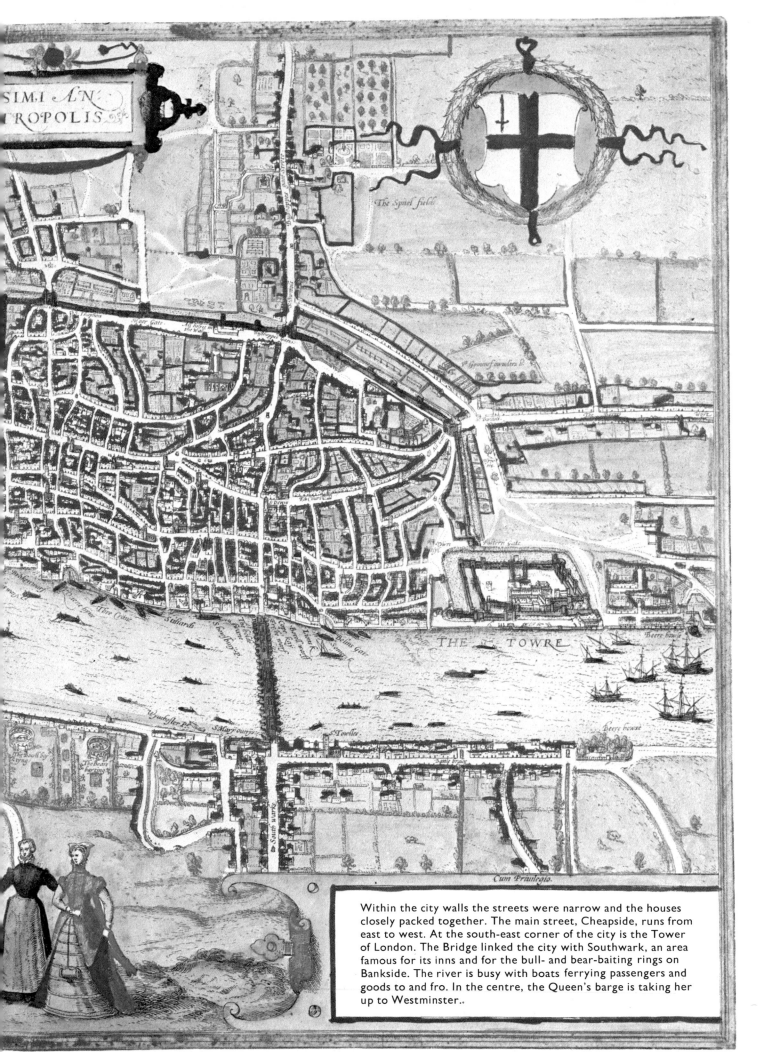

Within the city walls the streets were narrow and the houses closely packed together. The main street, Cheapside, runs from east to west. At the south-east corner of the city is the Tower of London. The Bridge linked the city with Southwark, an area famous for its inns and for the bull- and bear-baiting rings on Bankside. The river is busy with boats ferrying passengers and goods to and fro. In the centre, the Queen's barge is taking her up to Westminster..

# Tudor London

Tudor London was a prosperous and fashionable city. It acted like a magnet, drawing people to it from all over the country and even from abroad. Many thousands of people left the countryside and came to London in search of new opportunities. Young men came to serve apprenticeships or to study law at the Inns of Court. Foreign craftsmen set up workshops making articles such as clocks, glass and fine pottery. Industry was flourishing and goods were produced for the home market and for export. The presence of royalty and rich noblemen at the court at Westminster attracted painters, writers, actors and talented people of all kinds seeking recognition and fame.

With all these people flocking to London, the city became very overcrowded and more houses were built beyond the city wall. In the late 1530s Henry VIII closed the monasteries and the land of those in and around London also became available for building, but the city now had to run the hospitals and care for the old and the poor, which the religious orders had done in the past.

◄ Festivities in 16th century Bermondsey, then a small village across the river from the Tower of London. All sorts of people are there and more are arriving on horseback. Fashionably-dressed people stand in groups talking. In the centre, a man with a sword and buckler (shield) hands his cloak to a servant.

On the right, a procession of people dressed in black are arriving and in the foreground people are dancing. A long table is set for a feast and cooks are busy in the kitchen preparing food.

▲ "Fiddling knaves" in the Clink prison, a damp and notorious lock-up belonging to the Bishop of Winchester. It was not far from Bankside, near the bridge. We still sometimes talk of prisoners being "in clink."

◄ A picture map of Moorfields in 1558. It shows the city wall and a wide ditch beyond it. On the turrets of Moorgate rotting human heads warn would-be criminals of the fate that might await them. Paths lead across Moorfields where laundresses are laying out their washing to dry. An old woman appears to be having an argument with a man in a full suit of armour. In the next field citizens are practising their archery. On the right, small bridges lead into gardens with summer houses. In one corner of the field is a kennel.

THAMESIS

A view of Bankside, showing the Globe Theatre, the Bear Garden and the inns and taverns along the river. The Swan and the Rose theatres were nearby. Many actors and playwrights, including Shakespeare, took lodgings in this area.

▼A modern performance of Shakespeare's "Antony and Cleopatra". There are no longer any theatres on Bankside, but further up the river on the South Bank the National Theatre forms part of a new Arts Centre.

## The Elizabethan theatre

The theatre became very popular in Elizabethan London. Previously, plays had been performed at Court, in churches and churchyards and in the yards of inns. But now special theatres were being built, where companies of actors played to packed audiences. All the theatres were built outside the city to avoid regulations brought in by the city authorities, who felt that such gatherings attracted ruffians and pick-pockets and might spread diseases like the plague.

London's first theatre was built in Shoreditch in 1576. Twenty-one years later, the lease of the land it was built on ran out. The company acting there at the time was "The Lord Chamberlain's Men" and Shakespeare was one of its members. After trouble with the landlord, the company decided to take the wooden building down and put it up again over the river, on Bankside. They renamed it "The Globe". It opened in 1599 and many of Shakespeare's comedies and tragedies were performed there.

A flag flying from a theatre roof was a sign that there would be a performance at two o'clock in the afternoon. The crowds packed into the galleries and stood close together around the stage. The most expensive seats were stools on the stage itself. These were usually taken by fashionable young men who hoped to be noticed by everyone. The audiences were rowdy. They cracked nuts, sucked oranges, called out to each other, and interrupted the players. It was all part of the fun of going to the theatre.

The Globe was burned down in 1613, when a cannon mis-fired during a performance. One man's breeches caught fire, but luckily someone had some ale handy to put them out and everyone escaped unhurt. The Globe was rebuilt and remained in use until 1644.

# London's river

For centuries, the River Thames was London's link with the rest of the world. It was the route by which imports and exports passed through the city. Below the bridge was the stretch of river known as the "pool" where sea-going ships could anchor. Small boats called "lighters" ferried the cargoes between the ships and the various quays and wharves. In workshops and boatyards near the river, rope- and sail-makers, ship repairers and chandlers did a thriving trade. Many of Britain's sailing ships were built in the Thames shipyards.

Before London had buses and trains and several bridges over the river, the Thames was the city's main highway. It was quicker and more pleasant to travel by boat than to jostle with the crowds in the narrow streets. The river was crowded with the small boats of watermen who earned their living ferrying people to and fro. The watermen campaigned against the building of more bridges and became bitter enemies of the hackney carriage drivers and hirers of sedan chairs when they began operating in the city.

FLUVIUS

South Warke

▲ A view of London Bridge and the Thames in 1616 showing busy traffic on the river. The houses and shops on the bridge left only a narrow roadway for traffic. Heads of traitors were mounted on the gate-house at the southern end.

All along the water front were stairs and landing stages where people could get in and out of boats, fetch buckets of water, or simply sit and watch the world go by. At the various wharves and quays goods were loaded in and out of lighters.

◄ A sailing barge and rowing boats busy in the Pool of London towards the end of the 19th century.

▶ Today, the River Thames is no longer crowded and busy. Barges like these are becoming rare.

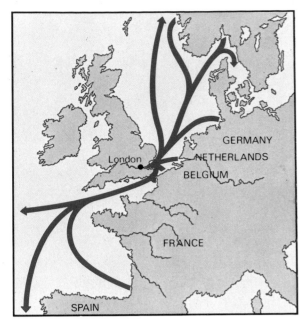

London grew up as a trading port because the Thames links it to routes to the continent and across the North Sea, to the Baltic and Russia and down to the Channel, to the rest of the world. From prehistoric times the Thames and the Rhine formed a trade route between Britain and the continent. In the Middle Ages, London exported wool and cloth to Europe. From the middle of the 16th century trading companies went further afield expanding Britain's trade. In the 19th century London became the centre of world trade.

## Shooting the bridge

Anyone wishing to hire a boat went down one of the steep lanes that led to the riverfront and summoned a passing waterman by calling "Oars! Oars!". In 1560, it cost a penny to cross the river and four pence to be ferried from the City to Westminster.

Until 1750 London only had one bridge. It presented special dangers to boats because the piers were so wide that they blocked the flow of the water. As the tide went out the water was held back. It dropped about a metre and a half as it poured through the arches and swirled in terrifying currents on the far side. Taking a boat through was called "shooting the bridge". Boats sometimes overturned and most passengers went ashore rather than risk drowning. The more daring enjoyed the thrill of narrowly missing the great piers as they were swept through the arches.

▲ The horseferry at Lambeth took carriages across the river to save them having to go right up to London Bridge. Outside the inn, a milk-maid is dancing to the music of a fiddler and boatmen sit drinking ale.

▼ A lively scene at Billingsgate fish market in 1808. Carts have come to collect fish which was unloaded from the fishing boats in the background. A fight has broken out and three stout fishwives watch with interest.

Medieval London Bridge stood for over six hundred years. It eventually became unsafe and in 1831 it was demolished. A new bridge designed by John Rennie was built. When Rennie's London Bridge was replaced by the present sleek concrete version, the old bridge was sold to America. Each stone was numbered as the bridge was carefully taken down and Rennie's London Bridge now stands in the new Lake Havasu City, Arizona.

### Fishing Bear
In 1252 Henry III was presented with a white bear by the King of Norway. It was kept in the Royal Menagerie at the Tower and was allowed to go fishing in the Thames on the end of a long, strong rope.

# Two terrible years

In the spring of 1665 plague broke out again in the crowded and filthy slums outside the city walls, but this time, as the weather became warmer the epidemic spread. Black rats carried the disease and their fleas passed it to humans. The signs were a high fever and swellings followed by the appearance of dark blotches under the skin called "tokens", which were a sign that death was near. People tried plague-waters and lucky charms, but there was no known cure and between 68,000 and 100,000 people died.

The following summer, 1666, the Great Fire devastated the city. It burned for four days and nights destroying 13,000 homes and leaving 100,000 people homeless. St Paul's Cathedral and 87 churches were burned out. The Royal Exchange and the halls of 44 city companies were destroyed. About four-fifths of the old medieval city within the walls was reduced to smouldering rubble, but the slums outside the city wall, where the plague had claimed most of its victims the year before, remained untouched.

### Four days that destroyed the city

The summer of 1666 was long and hot. Within the city wall, timber-framed houses stood closely packed together, their upper storeys overhanging the narrow streets and alleys. On the night of Saturday September 5th there was a strong east wind blowing. A fire broke out in a baker's shop in Pudding Lane. It quickly spread to the stables of the Star Inn nearby. From there it moved down towards the river where warehouses full of spirits, oil and hemp caught alight. Buckets of water, hand squirts and fire-hooks were useless against the blaze and the fire was soon completely out of control. It swept on and turned towards the centre of the city.

Samuel Pepys, the diarist, described the confusion as everyone tried to save their possessions. He said that the streets were "full of nothing but people and horses and carts loaded with goods, ready to run over one another and removing goods from one burned house to another". The air was filled with flames and smoke and the sound of cracking timber and falling buildings. King Charles himself rode around encouraging the teams of fire-fighters and even dismounted and helped.

On Tuesday evening, as darkness fell, the roof of St Paul's caught alight. The lead on the roof melted and ran down the stone walls. The roof beams gave way and stones and tombs split in the heat. In the crypt, hundreds of valuable books which had been taken there for safety were destroyed.

The next day sailors blew up rows of houses in an attempt to stop the fire spreading. The wind died down and the fire was gradually brought under control. By Thursday it was out, after burning for four days and nights. Very few lives were lost, but it was a sad sight that Londoners faced as they picked their way through the ash-covered ruins.

◄ Corpses of victims of the plague were buried in pits outside the city walls. In September, when the epidemic was at its height, over 7,000 people died in one week. At dawn and dusk the "deadcarts" rumbled through the deserted streets. The drivers clanged a bell and called out "Bring out your dead!" When someone died of the plague, the survivors were locked in their house for forty days. A large red cross was marked on the door and the words "Lord have mercy upon us" were written above it.

▲ Samuel Pepys was a Londoner who kept a diary from 1660 to 1669. It gives a detailed picture of life in London at the time. He described his work in the Navy Office, dinner parties, going to the theatre, buying a coach and trouble with his servants. He wrote about odd things that happened to him, such as the time his wig caught fire in Lord Burlington's house: "Here I also, standing by a candle that was brought for sealing of a letter, do set my perriwig a-fire, which made such an odd noise, nobody could tell what it was till they saw the flame."

◄ The Great Fire at its height. A fierce wind is sweeping the flames through the city. St Paul's is alight and the towers of gutted churches stand out against the reddened sky. Crowds of people escape by boat with piles of belongings.

# Wren's London

After the Great Fire, measures were immediately taken to help the thousands of homeless people who were camping in the fields around the city. Centres were set up for the storage of belongings and towns and villages had to take in Londoners. The task for clearing up and re-building had to begin as soon as possible. Several plans were put forward for re-building the city on a grand new scale. They would have been very expensive and individual property owners would have had to give up their rights. So in the end the city was re-built on the old street plan. Some streets were widened and all buildings had to be of brick and stone to reduce the risk of fire. Brick kilns were set up and timber was imported. Money was raised by a tax on coal. Most of the city was re-built within ten years.

The most brilliant architect to emerge was Christopher Wren. The great dome of St Paul's Cathedral and the varied spires and towers of his 51 City churches were unlike anything seen in England before. They added grace and interest to the skyline of the new city.

▲ A portrait of Sir Christopher Wren. He was Professor of Astronomy at Oxford and a brilliant mathematician. He taught himself architecture by studying buildings and plans and reading books. He became the country's leading architect.

▶ The new St Paul's Cathedral took 35 years to build. In this modern photograph of the floodlit cathedral, the massive dome seems almost weightless, but just the "lantern" and cross on top of the dome weigh 700 tons.

## Advances in science

In the late 17th century there was great interest in scientific discovery. Wren and Pepys were both members of the Royal Society where learned men met to watch experiments and exchange ideas. King Charles II was patron of the Society and went to its meetings. Charles II also founded a mathematical school and commissioned Wren to build the Royal Observatory at Greenwich.

Great advances were made in scientific knowledge. Instruments were developed to measure time and distance and to chart the movement of the stars. Maps and shipping charts became more accurate. Precision instruments and navigational aids were manufactured in London. Astronomers at Greenwich established the world's lines of longitude and latitude. Later it became the place from which world time is measured.

▼ The Monument to commemorate the Great Fire was put up near the spot where the fire started. Regular rows of brick or stone houses with tiled roofs and large windows replaced the untidy jumble of houses that had been destroyed.

▲ In the bitter winter of 1683-4 the Thames froze over for six weeks. A fair was held on the river. Watermen used oars and sails to make tents for sideshows. People had rides in boats on wheels and horse-drawn coaches drove on the ice.

## The Frost Fair

People came from all around London to visit the Frost Fair. Even King Charles II went to it. The gaily decorated booths sold food and drink, toys and souvenirs. One cunning cheat sold "diamond rings" made of ice. There was music and dancing. Puppet plays, performing monkeys, fire-eaters and sword-swallowers added to the fair-ground atmosphere.

◄ Bull-baiting was one of the many attractions on the ice. A whole ox was roasted and there was a fox hunt. People skated and played football and nine-pins. Everyone enjoyed the novelty of being at a fair on the frozen river.

▼ The sign for a house called "The Ape and Apple". Until house numbers were introduced in the 1760s many houses had signs as a means of identification.

► Until about 80 years ago the sounds in the streets of London were quite different from today. Above the rumble of cart wheels and the clatter of horses' hooves rose the cries of street traders advertising their wares. They went around selling food, clothes, toys, or household articles. Some repaired things like chairs or pots and pans.

25

# Georgian London

In the 18th century London grew in all directions, but especially westwards, towards Hyde Park. More and more people were moving out to live in the new suburbs, but the City remained London's business centre. Prosperous people usually moved west, as it was fashionable to live near the court. Some moved out to country villages like Hampstead or Kensington. New bridges opened up land south of the river. Poorer houses were put up to the east of the City for people who came to London to find work in the port or in the workshops and industries in the area.

There was no central organisation to run the city. The population rose above three quarters of a million and the old systems began to break down. The poor lived in filthy slums; thousands died of disease or in desperation took to drink or crime. Occasionally mob violence broke out. People began to realise that something must be done. Hospitals were built and efforts were made to improve the legal system and to curb crime.

◀ Grosvenor Square in 1789. The West End squares were built on the land of wealthy families like the Grosvenors and the Portmans. Elegant houses look out over a central garden. Raised pavements were a new introduction. The map below shows the Grosvenor Estate. Public hangings took place at Tyburn, near the present Marble Arch. Open fields lie north of Tyburn Road which is now Oxford St.

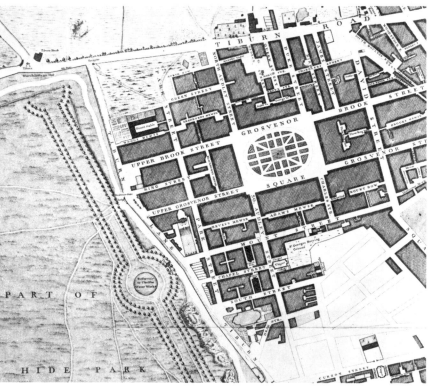

▲ Street lighting was introduced in the middle of the 18th century. Every evening lamp-lighters went round filling the lamps with whale oil and lighting the wicks.

▶ A fight at a gaming club. Pistols are drawn as the loser frantically holds onto his money. People in all classes of society gambled.

▼ Fashionable people at Vauxhall Pleasure Gardens walking under the lamplit trees while music floats down from an orchestra on the balcony. On summer evenings, it was pleasant to get out and enjoy fresh air and entertainment in one of the many pleasure gardens near the city.

▼ An artist called William Hogarth drew exaggerated pictures to make people notice what was going on around them. He called this picture "Night". The scene is a dark street near Charing Cross. A coach has been overturned and someone has thrown a burning torch into it. The two drunks do not even notice the coach or the two homeless people huddled asleep under the table near them. Nor do they realise what is about to land on their heads. The sign outside the barber's shop says "Shaving, Bleeding and Teeth Drawn with a Touch".

# The City: from coffee cups to computers

Voyages of discovery in the 16th century opened up sea routes all over the world. There was money to be made! Goods from far-off countries would sell in London at a profit. Groups of enterprising businessmen got together and formed trading companies to make the most of the new opportunities.

Nobody could finance these expensive ventures alone, so people lent money to the new companies in return for a share in the profits by buying stocks and shares. Merchants needed to charter ships. Ships and their cargoes could be lost at sea, so insurance developed. Once goods arrived they had to be sold, so markets or "exchanges" were set up. Backing all these activities were the banks. The most important was the Bank of England, founded in 1694. From the late 17th century onwards, modern business methods developed. Trade grew as Britain became the centre of a world empire. The industrial revolution brought a further boom and the City became the most important business centre in the world.

◄ Lively discussion going on in an 18th century coffee house. Customers sit smoking pipes and sipping dishes of coffee or chocolate. Waiters would run errands for customers. News sheets, and later newspapers, were provided.

▲ A tense moment during bidding at the Metal Exchange. Prices on this exchange are important in the supply of lead, tin, zinc, silver and copper to industry all over the world.

▲ The "floor" of the Stock Exchange really does look like a market as stock-brokers mill around the stands looking for the best prices for stocks and shares. The "floor" is directly linked to every major financial centre in the world.

## The coffee houses

Since the 16th century businessmen had met in a building called the Royal Exchange. But when coffee houses began to open in the late 17th century, those in the City became the centre of business life. Financiers met at Jonathan's and Garraway's. The coffee house of Mr. Edward Lloyd became the centre for shipping news and also the place to find merchants who insured ships and cargoes. In some coffee houses cargoes were auctioned "by the candle", which meant that bidding went on until one inch of a candle had burned down. Business eventually outgrew the coffee houses. By the end of the 18th century the various groups of businessmen were moving out into their own premises.

## The City today

Today, the Bank of England is the most important institution in the City. It is banker to the government and to all the main banks. It is the only bank in England allowed to issue notes. It also deals with the central banks of other countries and is internationally important. All the main British and foreign banks and merchant banks also have branches in the City. There are discount houses that deal in money and there is a money market and a gold market.

## Millions of pounds at stake

Lloyd's has developed from a coffee house into an international insurance market. Attendants here and in the Stock Exchange are still called "waiters". At Lloyd's, businessmen called underwriters share between them the enormous risk of insuring anything from jumbo jets to nuclear reactors. They will insure almost anything anywhere, from people running competitions for the capture of the Loch Ness monster, to a vehicle used on the moon.

## Ships and cargoes

The Baltic Exchange is the only international shipping exchange in the world. The transport of cargoes by sea and air is arranged here. It is also the market for grain and oil seeds. At the Commodity Exchange, the main things sold are sugar, rubber, cocoa, coffee and vegetable oils.

## Business based on trust

"My word is my bond" is the motto of the Stock Exchange and the Baltic Exchange. A deal worth millions of pounds is final once a man has given his word. The telex messages, computer calculations and contracts follow later. Much of the business in the City is done in this way. The City has a reputation for efficiency and reliability and it is still one of the leading business centres in the world.

▲ An aerial view of the City today with the Stock Exchange in the foreground. About 350,000 people work in the City, but only about 7,500 live there. Beyond St. Paul's, London stretches to the horizon.

▼ The Bank of England stores Britain's gold and some for other countries. In this vault, gold bars are being sorted before storage. Each bar is very heavy and is shaped so that it cannot be lifted in one hand.

# The docks

The number of ships bringing goods into London increased rapidly as Britain became the centre of a world empire. By the end of the 18th century, one company alone was sailing more ships than all the companies together had sailed a century earlier. The river was jammed with ships and lighters. There were not enough wharves and quays. This caused long delays as ships waited downstream, and cargoes were plundered by river thieves.

At the beginning of the 19th century, to overcome these problems, docks were built on the marshy land to the east of the City. They provided space for ships to unload and warehouses where goods could be stored in safety. The sale and distribution of the goods was organised in the City and London was the centre of world trade. By the end of the century, steam ships had taken over from sail. London was importing vast quantities of food and raw materials. Some were used by industry and a lot were re-exported, together with manufactured goods.

### River thieves

Before the docks were built, the River Thames was a forest of masts. Ships lay at anchor loaded with rum, sugar, coffee and tea—all goods that carried a high duty. Most of the crew were ashore and those left aboard could usually be bribed to keep silent. The valuable cargoes were rich plunder for the gangs of thieves who worked the river. There were plenty of people willing to act as receivers.

Gangs who worked at night were called "light horsemen". Under cover of darkness they boarded the ships with tools to open up the barrels of sugar and coffee. Using shovels, they filled sacks, called "black straps" as they were dyed black. They took a little from each barrel they opened, and then sealed them again. To steal rum, the gangs went aboard with pumps called "jiggers", tin tubes and devices to syphon the spirit from the barrels.

At daybreak the "heavy horsemen" moved in. They were usually "lumpers", the men who carried the casks from the ship's hold to the lighters. Their clothes had large hidden pockets that they filled with stolen goods. Once, while a ship's captain was searching the decks for some thieves, lumpers were down below passing his personal store of sugar out of a porthole into a waiting boat.

The gangs were often in league with the rat-catchers who went aboard ships at night to set traps. These men would even let rats go so that they could chase them into dark corners to collect loot hidden earlier by accomplices.

The thefts caused the shipping companies enormous losses until the building of the docks and the formation of the River Police put a stop to their activities.

▲ A view of the Thames showing one of the first docks, opened in 1805. Ships could now unload directly onto the quay. A high, prison-like wall enclosed the whole dock and armed guards protected the valuable cargoes in the warehouses.

▶ Inside an ivory warehouse in 1890. The London docks imported rare and expensive things from all over the world such as raw silk, furs, diamonds and ostrich feathers. Dealers from Europe came to the London ivory auctions.

▲ Midnight in the docks in the 19th century. A fight breaks out among dockers waiting outside a pub to be paid.

▼ Merchants inspecting a cargo of tea from China. Sailors from all over the world could be seen in London's docks.

▲ An aerial view of the docks shows their position between loops of the river. They stand almost empty now as most trade has moved to Tilbury, London's new port near the Thames estuary. The old docks are gradually being redeveloped.

◄ Modern machinery unloading a container ship at Tilbury, which is Britain's busiest sea port.

▼ St. Katherine's Dock, near the Tower of London, has been converted into a yacht marina and trade centre.

# Transport revolution

Changes in methods of transport in the 19th century had an enormous effect on London and the life of people living there. From the late 1830s onwards, London was linked by rail to the country's other great industrial centres, speeding up the movement of large quantities of goods. Letters, which from 1840 went by the new Penny Post, could be speeded to their destinations by rail. A network of railways grew up around the city and the built-up area spread rapidly as people moved out to live in the suburbs and travelled into work by train. Londoners who had never left the city were able to go on excursions to the country and to the seaside.

In the city and inner suburbs, an efficient system of public transport was developed. From the 1830s horse buses ran on regular routes and later horse-drawn trams ran outside central London. Roads were improved to cope with the increase in traffic. In the 1860s London got the world's first underground railway. New bridges were built and steam boats speeded up travel on the river.

▼ Hyde Park Corner in 1797 showing a toll gate in the distance. There is very little traffic. A lumbering waggon is making deep ruts in the muddy road surface. A coach loaded with passengers hurries towards Knightsbridge. Before horse buses were introduced, short-stage coaches carried passengers from the suburbs to inns in the City and West End. The fares were high and once in London they were not allowed to pick up or set down passengers except at the terminals. This was to prevent them taking custom away from the hackney coaches.

▶ Excited crowds watching a train on the London to Birmingham railway line as it comes out of the tunnel at Primrose Hill. In the middle of the 19th century everyone was mad about trains and railways. The amazing speed of the new method of travel opened up new horizons. Day excursions, both into and out of London were very popular. The big terminal stations were splendid buildings designed to be worthy of the new "railway age". Magnificent station hotels were built at the main terminals to accommodate passengers arriving in London.

◄ Inside the Bayswater omnibus. Along one side of the bus sit a nurse, a city gentleman, an elegantly dressed lady and a mother with two children. The bus has stopped near Hyde Park. There were no bus stops. People got on or off anywhere along the route.

▼ Top-hatted gentlemen enjoying a trial trip in contractor's waggons on the first underground line in 1862. It was called the Metropolitan Railway and ran from Paddington to the City. The trains were pulled by special steam engines.

## Horses everywhere

In the 1890s there were 300,000 working horses in London. Many were hired from men called jobmasters who kept hundreds of horses suitable for every kind of work. The tram and bus companies had large stables of horses. It took ten or eleven horses to keep each bus on the road. Each pair worked three and a half hours a day with one day's rest a week. Railway and shipping companies and carriers of goods also had large stables.

Horses came to London at four or five years old. They were usually well cared for, but the strain of the heavy London work wore them out in about five years. They were carefully chosen to suit the particular job. Brewers and refuse-collectors used very large, strong horses. Horses for private carriages had to be showy and well-behaved. Hansom cabmen liked brown horses. Greys were used at weddings and blacks at funerals.

◄ Horses resting at a cab stand in 1888. The four-wheeled cabs were known as "growlers". The two-wheeled hansom cabs were faster and more comfortable. In 1888 there were over 11,000 cabs in London. Cabs were expensive compared with trams or horse buses, but they took passengers right to their doorsteps.

► Traffic outside the Royal Exchange in the City in 1897. The streets are crowded with vehicles. There are delivery carts, hansom cabs and horse buses with passengers sitting on "garden seats" on the top.

# The spreading city

Once people were able to travel to work easily, there was no stopping the growth of London. Many people made enough money to move out of the centre of the city into comfortable houses in the suburbs. It was not only the size of London that grew faster than ever before. The industrial revolution was attracting more and more people to the cities to work and London's population rose from under two million in 1840 to four and a half million by 1900.

London was the world's largest industrial city. It made and used enormous quantities of goods. Thousands of people were employed in industries like engineering, furniture-making and the clothes and leather trades. There were also a vast number of service jobs—servants, shop assistants and delivery men.

In this huge mass of people the old problems like crime, poverty and disease became worse and worse. Eventually, the authorities were forced to take action. Many of the systems that keep London running smoothly today were set up in the 19th century.

▶ Haymakers in Canonbury fields in the 1780s. Villages were already being enlarged by the building of rows of houses, but the scene is still very rural.

▼ A 19th century artist's view of the spread of London. Trees scream and animals and haystacks flee in terror as the smoke and buildings spread.

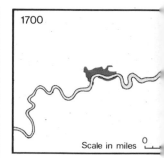

1700

Scale in miles

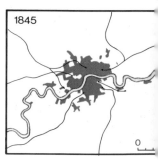

1845

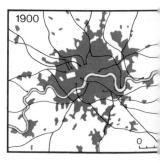

1900

▲ Maps showing the spread of London between 1700 and 1900. By 1845, London had spread across the river and was growing fast. But the real explosion took place in the next 50 years, with the growth of the railways and public transport.

▼ The figure of "Death" on the river Thames. All sewage went into the river. It was also the main source of drinking water. It spread deadly diseases.

▶ Thousands of people were made homeless by the building of railways through the built-up area. The houses nearby became grimy slums.

## Towards a safer city

1858 was the year of "the Great Stink". That summer the smell from the sewage in the Thames became unbearable. Diseases like typhoid and cholera lurked in the filthy waters. London desperately needed a proper sewage system. Soon after this main drains were built, but a clean water supply took longer.

Sir Robert Peel had founded the Metropolitan Police in 1829 and crime was at last being tackled. A centralised fire brigade was not organised until after a terrible warehouse fire in 1861 proved it was essential.

One person in three lived in desperate poverty in filthy, overcrowded slums. Reformers and charities made efforts to help, but it was a really gigantic problem. Large-scale improvements were not made until this century.

▼ The Victoria Embankment was built in the 1860s. A large wall was put up to hold back the river and the land between was made into a wide road. Underneath it pipes for gas and water (1), a main sewer (2) and an underground train tunnel (3) were built.

# Out and about in Victorian London

Victorian London had its problems, but there was also a brighter side to it. The city was the capital of a world empire. It was more prosperous than it had ever been before. Splendid and dignified new buildings reflected the capital's pride. The streets were full of bustle and the shops were crammed with all that anyone could desire. With the new public transport, it was easy to get about and there was so much to see and do.

People flocked to see new animals that arrived at the Zoo. They went to see the model of the earth's surface inside The Great Globe in Leicester Square. They went to the newly enlarged British Museum to wonder at its impressive collection of treasures. For pure entertainment, Astley's Amphitheatre was hard to beat. It combined circus and theatre in spectacular performances that included horses and chariots, battle scenes and amazing dramatic effects. There were also some fascinating curiosities to see. In 1886 an aquarium exhibited a so-called "living mermaid" in a tank full of fish.

▶ The Crystal Palace was an enormous building of iron and glass put up in Hyde Park for the Great Exhibition of 1851. It was designed by Joseph Paxton, head gardener of the Duke of Devonshire. The exhibition was intended to show "the works of industry of all nations" and the best ideas in art and design. After the exhibition the Crystal Palace was moved to South London.

▲ The Albert Memorial in Kensington Gardens was erected in memory of Prince Albert, Queen Victoria's husband, who died of typhoid in 1861. He was one of the main organisers of the Great Exhibition.

## The Great Exhibition

Six million people flocked to see the Crystal Palace and all the wonders displayed inside. In the centre was a crystal fountain, and the soaring arch of the roof enclosed three great trees. There were large working machines, raw materials, fascinating objects from the farthest corners of the earth, sculpture, ornaments and elaborately decorated furniture. There were also amazing inventions like a knife with 1,851 blades and the "silent alarum bedstead" that tipped "anyone out of bed at any given hour".

The Exhibition was a great success. The profits were used to encourage learning and good design, for which a large area of land was bought in Kensington. Here, museums of art, science and natural history and colleges of music and science were later built.

▲ An afternoon in Hyde Park. All sorts of people are enjoying the air. A smart lady shades her face with a parasol. Some ragged children have made a swing on the railings. There is boating on the Serpentine.

▼ A painting of the stars of late Victorian and Edwardian music hall. Londoners loved these variety shows and many of the songs became the 'pop' numbers of the day.

◄ A locksmith working in a London street. The cries of the traders added to the noise and bustle.

► A man with a dancing bear travels through the London suburbs. Street entertainers were a common sight in Victorian London. There were musicians, dancers, acrobats and Punch and Judy shows.

# London at war

When World War II broke out in September 1939, London was already preparing for the possibility of an air attack. At night strict black-out regulations were enforced so that the city would not show up to enemy aircraft.

The Blitz, Hitler's concentrated attack on the city, began on September 7th, 1940. He hoped to paralyse the capital and force an early end to the war. For 57 nights enemy bombers flew over the city dropping their deadly loads. By May 1941, when the Blitz ended, large areas of London lay devastated and in ruins. Especially hard hit were the City and the East End with its docks, warehouses, factories and power-stations.

From 1944 onwards Londoners had to face new weapons. These were the flying bombs or "doodlebugs" and the V2 rockets that were launched from the continent. The V2 rockets landed without warning and left no time to escape. By the end of the war 29,890 people in London had been killed and over 50,000 injured.

## Preparing for the war

London was divided into small areas with their own Air Raid Precaution posts. Gas masks and air-raid shelters were provided. People were told what to do if the sirens sounded. Searchlights and anti-aircraft guns were set up and barrage balloons tethered above the city. As Britain moved to the brink of war, children were evacuated to the country for safety.

▲ Entrance to a public air-raid shelter in the basement of a building. Sandbags protected buildings against bomb blasts.

◄ A soldier on leave says goodbye to his little son who is being evacuated from London with other children.

## Air raids

The first sign of an air raid was the wail of the sirens. Searchlights scanned the sky for enemy aircraft as they roared overhead. There were deafening explosions and the terrifying rumble of buildings collapsing. Fires raged. Firemen struggled to control the flames. The streets were filled with water, rubble and glass. Then there was the searching for the injured—and the dead.

▲ Preparing vegetable plots near the Albert Memorial as part of the "Dig for Victory" campaign.

► Crowds sleeping on the platform of an underground station. Conditions were dreadful, but at least people felt safe.

## Londoners unite

Londoners were determined not to let the bombing get them down. Many of them lost their homes and possessions or had neighbours or relatives killed or injured. Some had the added worry of sons and husbands fighting in the forces. Yet they carried on as normally as possible and even managed to joke about the war. Their courage was admired by the whole world.

▲ Men inspecting damage in a library after it had been hit by incendiary bombs. These small bombs were showered out of planes and were designed to start fires. In this case much damage was also caused by the water used to put out the fire.

◄ A flying bomb has just fallen in a street in the middle of the day. Heavy rescue workers—trained to go into unsafe buildings —are on the scene. Passers-by are helping with an injured man on a stretcher.

## V.E. Day

Victory in Europe was announced on 8th May, 1945. Huge crowds gathered outside Buckingham Palace to see the royal family and Winston Churchill. When darkness fell every possible light was switched on to celebrate the end of nearly six years of black-out. Pubs were drunk dry and everyone celebrated. It was the end of the war for London.

▲ Helpers standing among the remains of Farringdon Market Place where a V2 rocket fell, killing 380 people. It was the last bomb to fall on London.

► The flags were out on V.E. Day and everyone in London celebrated the end of the war.

# The East End

The East End grew up with the spread of industries to the east of the City and the growth of the port and the docks. It covers a wide area. A part like Bethnal Green, which was once a country village, is quite different from the area down by the river.

People living in the East End usually worked near their homes. It is also one of the areas of London where people from abroad have settled in the hope of finding work. For centuries, foreigners have made London their home. Some have been forced to leave their own countries for religious or political reasons. Others have come in the hope of making a better life. Some brought new skills and started new industries.

London's industries have usually been carried on in a large number of small workshops and factories rather than in enormous factories and mills. Recently, many industries have moved out of the East End. As a result, large areas, including some of the docks, are going to be redeveloped.

◀ A Jewish delicatessen in Wentworth Street. The East End has a large Jewish population.

▶ A pleater at work in a clothing factory. The East End has always been one of the centres of London's clothing industry.

▲ Petticoat Lane Market takes place every Sunday morning. There are hundreds of stalls and it has become one of the sights of London. Men demonstrate wonder kitchen gadgets and stall-holders attract customers with shouts of "Fantastic bargain!" "Beautiful quality! Pay twice the price up the West End!"

▶ An artist's impression of a winter evening in an East End street. Fruit and vegetables are being sold from roadside barrows and a man is roasting chestnuts. The shops are small family businesses. The butcher and shoe-mender are serving their last customers. The fish and chip shop already has a long queue.

▲ Moslems going to worship in an East End mosque. This building has changed its use as different people have come to live in the area. It started as a church for French Protestant silk-weavers in the 17th century and has also been a synagogue.

▲ Many streets of small houses in the East End have now been swept away and replaced by blocks of high-rise flats. Families do not like these because children have nowhere to play except the stairways and corridors, or right down at ground level. Many people also find these blocks very lonely and vandals cause damage. As a result, councils are building no more high-rise flats.

◄ Bells being made at the Whitechapel Bell Foundry. This foundry started in 1570 and is one of the only two remaining bell foundries in the country. It makes bells for churches all over the world. One of the most famous bells cast here was Big Ben. It weighs over $13\frac{1}{2}$ tons.

**Cockney rhyming slang**
A dialect has grown up in the East End known as "rhyming slang" because words are replaced with other words or phrases which rhyme. For instance, "apples and pears" means "stairs". Other examples are:

    Plates of meat = feet
    Mince pies = eyes
    Dog and bone = 'phone
    Gregory Peck = neck
    Boat race = face
    Barnet Fair = hair

However, usually only the first word of the phrase is used, e.g. "Use your loaf" is short for "Use your loaf (of bread)" which means "Use your head".

Costermongers are men who sell vegetables and fruit from barrows. In the 19th century, they sometimes used "backward slang" so they could speak to each other without other people understanding, e.g.: "Cool the esclop!" was "Look, the police!" backwards.

# Westminster

An abbey and a royal palace were built at Westminster in the 11th century. Later kings extended the palace and made it their main residence. Westminster became the centre of government and justice.

Westminster Hall was begun by William II in 1097. Medieval kings used the hall as part of their palace. They held councils and State ceremonies there. At Coronation feasts the King's Champion, dressed in full armour, used to ride into the hall on a magnificent horse. He challenged anyone who dared to question the king's right to the throne to come forward for combat.

From the 13th century, the Courts of Justice were held in Westminster Hall. In Pepys's time it was always crowded with people watching the proceedings. Foreigners were amazed to see the lawyers in their wigs and black gowns. Around the hall, stalls sold articles such as books, quill pens, gloves, ribbons and toys. Afterwards, visitors could refresh themselves at one of the taverns or eating houses nearby. The Heaven and Hell taverns were always popular.

▲ The coronation of Henry IV. With two exceptions, every monarch since Harold in 1066 has been crowned at Westminster Abbey.

## Westminster Abbey

Westminster Abbey was founded in the 11th century by Edward the Confessor. He was a very religious king who had vowed to make a pilgrimage to Rome. He was unable to do this and so he decided to build a great abbey at Westminster instead.

Two centuries later, the first abbey was demolished and was replaced by the present one. It has tall, pointed arches, beautiful stained glass windows and magnificent tombs.

The Abbey has always been closely connected with royalty. Coronations and royal weddings are held there. Many famous people are buried there including kings and queens, statesmen, poets, musicians and writers.

► Edward I and his Parliament. The king has summoned the "Lords Spiritual" who are wearing their bishops' mitres; the "Lords Temporal", or peers, in their fur trimmed robes; and the Commons, representatives of the various communities. In the centre are the woolsacks, symbols of the wealth of medieval England. Later, the Commons and the Lords began meeting separately, as they do today. Over the centuries, power gradually passed from the monarch to Parliament, but the idea behind it goes back to the 13th century.

▼ The chamber of the House of Commons today. The Government and Opposition sit on opposite sides of the chamber. During debates, no M.P. is allowed to step over the red lines that run down the edges of the carpet. By tradition they are two sword lengths apart.

▲ In 1834 the old Houses of Parliament were destroyed by fire. They were replaced by the present Houses of Parliament. Westminster Hall was saved.

► Demonstrators presenting a petition at the entrance to the Houses of Parliament.

◄ An aerial view of Westminster today showing:
1. The Abbey.
2. Westminster Hall.
3. The House of Lords.
4. The House of Commons.
5. Big Ben.

# Royal London

London's close connection with the Crown gave it a lead over every other city in England. The settling of government at Westminster made London the capital. The splendour of the Court made London especially fashionable. But the City resented any royal interference in its affairs. So when kings wanted money or support, the City bargained for powers of self-government.

There are several royal palaces in London and some of the parks were once royal hunting grounds. The Tudor palace of Whitehall no longer exists. It was a rambling collection of buildings, but inside it was richly decorated. It had fine paintings and tapestries and a library of velvet-covered books, some studded with pearls and jewels.

Buckingham Palace started as a fine brick mansion built by the Duke of Buckingham in 1703. It looked majestically out over St James's Park. Envious royal eyes were turned on it from St James's Palace nearby. George III bought it to use as a private house. Queen Victoria was the first sovereign to use it as an official palace.

▲ The Coronation procession of Edward VI passing through London as it goes from the Tower to Westminster in 1547. All along Cheapside crowds are watching from decorated stands. At special royal celebrations, the main pumps in the city flowed with wine.

▶ Crowds watching the execution of Charles I outside the Banqueting House in Whitehall in 1649. Charles I had quarrelled with Parliament. It led to the Civil War in which London took the side of Parliament.

▶ The state opening of Parliament takes place at the beginning of every parliamentary year. The Queen, as head of state, sits on the throne wearing the Parliamentary robe and Imperial State Crown. Sitting on woolsacks directly in front of her are the judges. On the main benches are the bishops and peers—the Lords Spiritual and Temporal—in their scarlet robes. Members of the House of Commons and diplomats are also present. The Queen reads a speech which sets out the Government's programme for the year.

◀ The Queen leaving Buckingham Palace in the golden State Coach at the start of her Silver Jubilee procession. Television may give a good view of royal processions, but it cannot convey the atmosphere and thrill of actually being there.

▼ The Tower of London has stood for 900 years. It was begun by William the Conqueror. Royal apartments, walls, towers and a moat were added to the original White Tower by various kings, making it one of the strongest fortresses in England.

## The Tower of London

William the Conqueror began building the White Tower in the late 1070s. He did not trust the population of London, so the Tower was intended both to defend the city and to remind Londoners of his military strength. Until the 17th century the Tower was a royal palace. It was the custom for sovereigns to spend the night before their coronation in the Tower. They then rode in procession right through the city to Westminster.

The Tower also became a state prison. Some prisoners faced tortures such as the rack, and many were executed in front of bloodthirsty crowds on Tower Hill. A few were beheaded on Tower Green away from the public gaze. Many famous people were imprisoned there. One prisoner made a daring escape disguised as a woman. Another climbed to freedom down a rope, smuggled to him in a container of wine.

The crown jewels are kept in the Tower. In 1671 some of them were nearly stolen by a Colonel Blood. He masqueraded as a clergyman and gained the confidence of the custodian. He and his accomplices were captured as they made their getaway.

The Tower also used to house the royal menagerie, the royal mint and the royal armoury. In the White Tower there is still an amazing collection of weapons and armour to be seen.

# Capital City

London is the capital of Great Britain. This strictly means that it is the seat of the country's government. Because of this, it is also the centre of law and administration and is the city where foreign countries have their embassies.

But London is also the capital in a much wider sense. It is the country's largest city and is the main business centre. It is the focus of the country's transport and communications systems. It has the busiest port and airport and is at the centre of the rail and road networks. The national radio, television and press centres are in London. It is linked to the rest of the world by the most advanced telecommunications.

London is also the country's arts and entertainment capital. It is famous for its many theatres and concert halls and has the nation's main art galleries and museums. In the sports sphere, thousands of enthusiasts watch national and international sporting events at places like Wembley, Twickenham, Wimbledon, Lords and the Oval.

◀ London as the centre of justice. A barrister leaves the Royal Courts of Justice. The country's highest courts are in London. Criminals are tried at the Old Bailey. The House of Lords is the final court of appeal in the country.

▼ Arts capital. Fun at the last night of the Proms at the Albert Hall. There are no seats in the stalls at Promenade concerts. It has become traditional to wave flags and sing patriotic songs at the last concert in each series.

► London as a sports and entertainment capital. Wembley Stadium holds 100,000 people and is the place where the football Cup Final is held. Here, fans have gathered for a pop concert.

▲ London as the centre of the country's government. A light shining at night in the tower above Big Ben is a sign that the politicians in the House of Commons are still sitting.

▼ Press capital. Lorries delivering bales of newspaper near Fleet Street, where the national newspapers are published. The papers are printed at night so that they are ready for early morning delivery.

► London as an exhibition centre. The Smithfield show being held in one of London's exhibition halls. People like to combine a visit to an exhibition with a day or two in London.

# Feeding the seven million

Nearly seven million people live in London. It is difficult to imagine how much food seven million people eat. As an example—if every household in London ate a pound of sausages a week, in four months, enough sausages would be bought to stretch right around the world at the equator.

There are several specialised wholesale food markets in London. Much food is imported and the markets supply other parts of the country as well as London. Smithfield deals with meat, New Covent Garden with fruit and vegetables, and Billingsgate with fish.

London has a great number and variety of places to eat out. They range from hamburger bars to famous restaurants. There are foreign restaurants of every nationality which serve dishes cooked by real experts. Many up-and-coming chefs train in the top hotels.

Then there are all the banquets. They are very splendid occasions. The long tables glitter with silver and candles and the guests are often very distinguished people.

▼ Lunchtime in a Lyon's Corner House in the 1930s. The waitresses were called "nippies". These restaurants were very popular because they provided inexpensive meals in smart surroundings. The really rich went to places like the Ritz.

◄ A 1930s cartoon of a scene in Simpson's, a very smart London restaurant. The customer is asking if the meat is English or foreign. Everyone is horrified that he should dare to suggest that it could be anything but the very best English beef.

▲ The Lord Mayor's dinner for Her Majesty's Judges is held once a year in the Mansion House, his official residence. Behind the Lord Mayor are the mace and the state sword of the City.

► Fruit and vegetables from all over the world can be bought in London. Here, a group of West Indian women are carefully examining tropical fruit for sale on a market stall.

▲ Smithfield Market in 1831. Some of the cattle look slightly out of control. Until 1855 animals were driven through the streets to Smithfield. In 1868, an indoor meat market opened on the same site.

▶ Large container lorries arriving at night at New Covent Garden Market, south of the river. The market's move from its old site in Central London has cut down traffic congestion.

◀ London's wholesale fish market at Billingsgate. Trading in all the wholesale markets begins very early in the morning so that people who want food to sell that day can get their supplies.

▶ An Italian food shop crammed with a huge range of pastas, cheeses, wines and other specialities. London has food shops catering for almost every nationality.

# A shopper's paradise

London has an amazing number and variety of places to shop. They range from market stalls to some of the most luxurious shops and department stores in the world. Where you shop and what you buy depends on your interests—and the size of your bank balance. You can buy anything in London from a cheap plastic spoon to a necklace set with diamonds and emeralds costing £60,000.

There are glossy department stores and huge chain stores crowded with shoppers from all over the world. There are modern, up-to-the-minute shops throbbing with music and full of the latest fashions. There are small shops that specialise in one thing. It may be chandeliers, or tropical fish or hand-made hats. In quiet back streets, often in just one room on the first floor of a building, there are combined shops and workshops where you can get things like replacement hands for an old grandfather clock, or spare parts for a model railway. The street markets sell food, clothes and household goods. Some specialise in antiques.

◀ A traffic jam in Oxford Street in 1928. Motor traffic was introduced at the beginning of the century and soon replaced horse-drawn vehicles. For two hundred years Oxford Street has been one of London's main shopping streets.

▶ An Arab man and woman shopping in a department store. London has become a cheap shopping centre for many foreign visitors. Many shops will arrange to have goods sent abroad for foreign customers.

◀ Harrods is one of the most famous stores in the world. It offers enormous choice. A man can choose from 500 different shirts and 9,000 ties, a woman from 8,000 dresses. The food halls still look much as they did in Edwardian times.

▼ Bond Street is just off Oxford Street. In contrast to the massive crowds and huge stores in Oxford Street, most of the shops here are small and sell beautiful and expensive things. There are dress shops, jewellers and picture galleries.

◀ London is the centre of the international art and antique market. This sale at Sotheby's of a private collection of art treasures from Europe raised nearly £18.5 million. The sign above the auctioneer converts bids into six currencies. The saleroom was linked by telephone to cities as far apart as Tokyo and Los Angeles so that buyers there could bid against people actually at the sale.

▼ A far cry from Sotheby's, the antique market in Portobello Road is held every Saturday. The street is crowded with people looking for bargains amongst the furniture, glass, pictures, silver, china and old clothes.

▲ James Smith and Sons, Umbrella Makers. Established 1830. Many of these small specialist shops still look very much as they did a hundred years ago. They pride themselves on the personal service they give their customers.

51

# The changing face of London

Since the war, large areas of London have been redeveloped. Giant tower blocks of offices and flats and enormous hotels make all the older buildings seem small. In the City, a new residential area called the Barbican has been developed and on the South Bank there is a new Arts Centre. New motorways, roads and undergrounds have speeded up travel. Pollution of the Thames is being reduced and fish, including salmon, are returning.

But are we making mistakes? Are too many old buildings being destroyed? Do people like living and working in enormous buildings? Is the new architecture interesting? Will all the concrete being used become dull and shabby with age? Can we go on allowing more and more cars into central London? Does London make enough of its river? If we want really exciting schemes, how will we pay for them?

The planners realise that decisions made now will shape London for the next century, or even longer. A city is for people. The question is—what sort of city do people want?

▼ A bus and an inspector with a flare in the smog of 1952. London's air used to be full of smoke from thousands of chimneys. Smoke and dirt combined with fog to produce a thick "smog". People with weak chests found it difficult to breathe and some even died.

▶ London seen across the river from the South Bank Arts Centre. London is now a smokeless zone. The air is much cleaner and smogs do not occur any more. Many of the older buildings that were covered with a thick layer of soot and grime have been cleaned.

 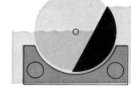

▲ Gates resting in concrete sills on river bed.

▲ Gate being raised against flood water.

▲ Gate fully raised in flood position.

### The Thames Barrier

The world's largest moveable barrier is being built across the Thames at Woolwich to protect London from flood dangers. High tide levels are rising and the combination of an ocean surge, a gale and a high tide might force a mass of water up the Thames. A million people and 45 square miles of London might be at risk. The red area on the map shows the area which might be affected.

The barrier is an amazing feat of engineering. It consists of a series of moveable steel gates set between nine piers in the river. Normally the gates will rest in sills in the river bed. If there is danger of a flood, they will be raised by machinery in the piers to form a solid barrier right across the river to hold the water back. Downstream of the barrier the river banks are being raised and strengthened. The G.L.C. are responsible for the project.

# Fly the Tube

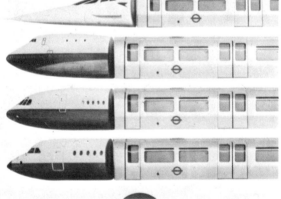

▲ A London Transport advertisement for the new extension of the Underground system that links Heathrow Airport directly to central London. 26 million passengers a year use Heathrow. New York is only 3½ hours away by Concorde.

◄ The countryside around London is now part of what is called the Green Belt, which has very strict building controls to stop London spreading any further.

▶ A street near Notting Hill Gate as it used to be and as it is now. A hundred years ago, houses in this area were let to people like grooms, laundresses, breeches-makers and dress-makers. Some houses had over twenty people living in them. Within the last 30 years, these houses have become expensive and are now occupied by executives and professional people. Large areas of London have changed in this way.

# When?

**ROMAN 43 A.D.–410.** Invasion 43 A.D. Bridge over Thames. London grew up at bridgehead. After 60 A.D. replaced Colchester as capital. By 410 Roman army withdrawn.

**5th–11th CENTURIES.** 5th and 6th centuries, Saxons settled in Britain. By 7th century London the chief town of East Saxons. Trade recovered. Late 8th century, beginning of Viking raids. End 10th century, Danish attacks. London centre of resistance.

**MEDIEVAL 1066–1485.** Population in 14th century about 40,000. 13th century London becoming political and administrative capital of country. First Parliaments. Increased trade. Rise of guilds. Influence of Church. Powers of self-government extracted by the City from Crown.

**TUDOR 1484–1603.** Population 1530: about 50,000. 1600: about 200,000. City overcrowded, spread. Dissolution of monasteries led to need to organise social services. Immigrants started new industries. Second half 16th century formation of trading companies, expansion of trade. 1576 birth of the theatres.

**17th CENTURY.** Population end 17th century 6–700,000. By mid-century suburbs reach Holborn and Westminster. 1660s: Bloomsbury, St James's, latter becoming fashionable court suburb. Re-building of City in brick and stone after Fire. Second half century imports from all over world influencing furniture, dress, food. Coffee houses centres of news, social and business life. Beginnings of City institutions: 1662 Royal Society, 1694 Bank of England.

**18th CENTURY.** Population over 900,000 by end of century. City spread in all directions especially West. Contrast riches of few and desperate poverty of majority. Old systems inadequate. Reforms left to individuals and charity. Luxury trades—furniture porcelain, watches, silk. Pleasure gardens. London important centre of European music. 1768, the Royal Academy. Growth of trade. Congestion of Thames. Further development of banking and insurance.

**19th CENTURY.** Population 1841: nearly 2 million; 1900: about 4½ million. Industrial revolution. From 1830s transport revolution. Rapid growth in size of city. Urban problems so bad that extensive solutions had to be organised by central authorities: 1829, Metropolitan Police; from 1859 main drains; 1866 Metropolitan Fire Brigade. London capital of world empire. Centre of world trade organised in City. 1870s Board Schools.

**20th CENTURY.** Present population just under 7 million. Further spread led to creation of Green Belt in 1930s. Development of facilities for large numbers of people: chain stores, sports stadia, cinemas, restaurants, large hotels. Slum clearance and relief of poverty. From 1960s development of Tilbury as London's port. London no longer the centre of an empire or leading city in the world, but "the City" is still one of the world's most important business centres.

# Where?

**70–125:** Fine public buildings including basilica and forum, governor's palace. **Early 2nd century:** Cripplegate fort. About **200 A.D.:** city wall. **4th century:** riverside wall.

**604:** Founding of St Paul's Cathedral. Westminster: monastery founded in **8th century**. King Cnut (1016–1035) built palace at Westminster; burned down **1036**. Edward the Confessor (1042–1066) built palace and Abbey, latter consecrated **1065**.

**1078:** White Tower begun. Westminster Hall **1097** (roof 14th century). **1176–1209:** London bridge built in stone. **1087–1327:** St Paul's re-built. **1123:** St Bartholomew's, **1213:** St Thomas's Hospitals. **13th century:** beginning of re-building of Westminster Abbey. **1411:** Guildhall begun.

**1512:** Fire destroyed royal apartments of Palace of Westminster. **1514:** Hampton Court Palace. **1529:** Henry VIII acquired York Palace; extended it and re-named it Whitehall Palace. **1528:** St James's Palace. **1569:** Royal Exchange built as meeting place for businessmen and merchants. **1599–1644:** The Globe Theatre.

**1619:** Banqueting House and **1630s:** Covent Garden, London's first square, by Inigo Jones. **1670–86:** City churches; **1675–1710:** St Paul's Cathedral; **1675:** Royal Observatory; **1682–92:** Royal Hospital, Chelsea, all by Wren. **1689:** Kensington House bought by William III, converted to Palace by Wren. **1694–1705:** Greenwich Hospital, now Royal Naval College, designed by Wren and Hawksmoor. **1698:** Whitehall Palace destroyed by fire.

**First half 18th century:** St George's, Guy's, Middlesex and Foundling Hospitals. **1750:** Westminster Bridge, the first of several new bridges. **1753:** the Mansion House, official residence of the Lord Mayor. **1756:** the New Road, London's first by-pass (now Marylebone, Euston and Pentonville Roads). **1759:** Royal Botanic Gardens, Kew. **1768:** The Adelphi by Adam Bros. Second half of century: gentlemen's clubs in St James's, developed from coffee houses.

**From 1802** docks: for unloading cargoes. **1812–30:** Regency improvements, most important of which was Regent's St. **1826–30:** Trafalgar Square. **1825–35:** Belgravia. **1823:** beginning of re-building of British Museum. **1831:** medieval London Bridge replaced. **1837:** Euston, London's first main line railway station. **1840:** Barry's Houses of Parliament begun. **1851:** Crystal Palace. **From 1856:** museums etc. in South Kensington. **1860s:** the Embankment.

**Mid 1920s:** Croydon airport. **1924:** Wembley. **1944:** Heathrow Airport. **1952:** Royal Festival Hall. Redevelopment of large areas after bomb damage of World War II. **1965:** G.P.O. Tower. **1960–70s:** the Barbican and the South Bank Arts Centre. Thamesmead, a completely new town on the edge of London, an experiment in planning. Due for completion **early 1980s:** Thames Barrier. Scheduled for redevelopment: large areas of the East End.

# What?

**60 A.D.:** *Londinium* destroyed in the rebellion of Queen Boudicca.

**851:** London sacked by Vikings. **886:** Alfred, King of Wessex, regained and fortified London. **1016:** Danish King Cnut accepted.

**1066:** Norman Conquest. **1349:** The Black Death. **1381:** Peasants' Revolt. **1476:** William Caxton, printing press in Westminster.

Reformation. Dissolution of monasteries by Henry VIII in late **1530s**.

**1605:** Gunpowder Plot. **1642–9:** Civil War. **1649–1660:** Commonwealth. **1660:** Restoration of Monarchy. **1665:** Great Plague. **1666:** Great Fire. **1684:** Frost Fair: most famous of the Thames frost fairs.

**1720:** South Sea Bubble: a financial disaster. **1780:** The Gordon Riots: a week of violent anti-Catholic riots; Newgate prison burned; troops brought out. **1784:** Lunardi's balloon ascent from Moorfields.

**1806:** Nelson's funeral. **1820:** Cato St. Conspiracy. **1834:** Burning of Houses of Parliament. **1851:** The Great Exhibition. **1861:** Tooley St. fire. **Late 1880s:** Workers' demonstrations. **1897:** Diamond Jubilee.

**Pre-1914:** Violent Suffragette demonstrations. **1914–18:** World War I. **1926:** General Strike. **1939–45:** World War II. **1940–41:** The Blitz. **1952:** Festival of Britain. **1977:** Silver Jubilee.

# Who?

## Famous people in London

**Rahere** (died 1144): Founded St Bartholomew's Hospital and Priory after the Saint appeared to him in a vision when he fell seriously ill on pilgrimage to Rome.

**Thomas Becket** (1118–70): Born London. Archbishop of Canterbury. Murdered. One of London's saints.

**Geoffrey Chaucer** (c. 1343–1400): Son of a London wine-merchant. Became courtier, diplomat and Controller of Customs and Subsidies on Wools, Skins and Hides in the Port of London. Author of The Canterbury Tales.

**Sir Thomas More** (1478–1535): Scholar and statesman. Lived in Chelsea.

**Richard Burbage** (1567–1619) and **Edward Alleyn** (1566–1626): Famous actors in Shakespeare's time. Alleyn founded Dulwich College.

**Christopher Marlowe** (1564–93): Playwright.

**Sir Thomas Gresham** (1519–79): Merchant and financier. Prime mover in the building of the Royal Exchange.

**Inigo Jones** (1573–1652): Architect. Born in London. Introduced classical architecture. Banqueting Hall.

**William Harvey** (1578–1657): Physician at St Bartholomew's Hospital. Discovered circulation of the blood.

**Samuel Pepys** (1633–1703): Born London. Diarist. Worked as Navy clerk, and secretary to the Admiralty. Moved easily in Court circles. President Royal Society.

**John Evelyn** (1620–1706): Diarist and author.

**Sir Christopher Wren** (1632–1723): Astronomer, architect. (See page 24.)

**Robert Hooke** (1635–1703): Chemist and physicist. City surveyor after Great Fire. Prominent member of Royal Society.

**Nicholas Hawksmoor** (1661–1736): Architect. Pupil of Wren.

**Jack Sheppard** (1702–24): Notorious robber and prison breaker, highwayman.

**George Frederic Handel** (1685–1759): Lived in London from 1712. Principal Court Composer to George I.

**William Hogarth** (1697–1764): Painter and engraver.

**Henry Fielding** the novelist and his blind half-brother **John Fielding** magistrates at Bow St Court 1748–54 and 1751–80. Organised band of paid constables, eventually known as Bow St Runners.

**David Garrick** (1717–79): Actor-manager Drury Lane.

**Robert Adam** (1728–92): Architect.

**Chippendale** and **Hepplewhite**: famous furniture makers who worked in London in the second half of the 18th century.

**John Nash** (1752–1835): Regency architect.

**Humphrey Davy** (1778–1829): Chemist and President of the Royal Institution. His assistant, **Michael Faraday** (1791–1867), made important discoveries in chemistry and physics.

**Elizabeth Fry** (1780–1845): Horrified by conditions in Newgate prison. Prison reformer.

**Edwin Chadwick** (1800–90): Social reformer. Worked for improvement in sanitation and public health.

**William Booth** (1829–1912): Evangelist. Founder of the Salvation Army which began in the East End of London.

**Dr Barnardo** (1845–1905): Worked among destitute children in the East End.

**Sir Arthur Conan Doyle** (1850–1930): Creator of Sherlock Holmes, the fictional Baker St detective.

## Monarchs from 1066

William I (1066–1087)
William II (1087–1100)
Henry I (1100–1135)
Stephen (1135–1154)
Henry II (1154–1189)
Richard I (1189–1199)
John (1199–1216)
Henry III (1216–1272)
Edward I (1272–1307)
Edward II (1307–1327)
Edward III (1327–1377)
Richard II (1377–1399)
Henry IV (1399–1413)
Henry V (1413–1422)
Henry VI (1422–1461)
Edward IV (1461–1483)
Edward V (1483)
Richard III (1483–1485)
Henry VII (1485–1509)
Henry VIII (1509–1547)
Edward VI (1547–1553)
Mary I (1553–1558)
Elizabeth I (1558–1603)
James I (VI of Scotland) (1603–1625)
Charles I (1625–1649) beheaded
Commonwealth (1649–1660)
Charles II (1660–1685)
James II (VII of Scotland) (1685–1688)
William III (1689–1702)
Mary II (1689–1694)
Anne (1702–1714)
George I (1714–1727)
George II (1727–1760)
George III (1760–1820)
George IV (1820–1830)
William IV (1830–1837)
Victoria (1837–1901)
Edward VII (1901–1910)
George V (1910–1936)
Edward VIII (1936) abdicated
George VI (1936–1952)
Elizabeth II (Acceded 1952)

## London characters

**DICK WHITTINGTON** (c.1360–1423) was the son of a Gloucestershire knight. He was apprenticed to a London mercer (merchant). He became a prosperous merchant himself and was Mayor of London four times. He left large sums of money to charity. Legends about his cat and about Bow Bells calling him back to London as he sat on Highgate Hill, grew up long after his death.

**JOHN STOW** (1525–1605): Tailor and historian. Wrote a Survey of London which was published in 1598. In it he describes the different areas of London and adds details about the history, people and customs. In commenting on the spread of London that had occurred in his lifetime, he sadly mentioned that armourers' workshops and storehouses had replaced a farm where, as a boy, he used to go and get milk "hot from the cows" at a halfpenny for three pints. There is a monument to Stow in the church of St Mary Undershaft in the City. Every year, at a special ceremony, the quill pen in the statue's hand is renewed.

**JOHN TAYLOR** (1580–1613) was a Thames waterman who wrote lively verses about life on the river. He became known as "the Water Poet". Like many other Thames watermen, he was "pressed" into the navy several times. He helped campaign against what he called the "hired hackney hell carts" that the watermen felt were a threat to their livelihoods.

Taylor was sponsored on several crazy publicity stunts. On one occasion, he and a friend nearly drowned when they rowed from London to the Kent coast in a boat made of brown paper.

**THOMAS DOGGETT** was a comic actor. He was delighted when George I of the House of Hanover succeeded to the throne of England. In 1715, to celebrate the event, he presented an orange coat with a silver badge as a prize for a rowing race. Only young men who had recently completed their apprenticeships and become members of the Watermens Company were able to compete.

**SAMUEL JOHNSON** (1709–1784): Writer and essayist. He lived near Fleet St. He was a very large and ugly man, but a brilliant talker. He was a member of London's literary circle and a friend of Oliver Goldsmith, the playwright, and Joshua Reynolds, the portrait painter. He compiled a dictionary, a task which took him eight years. He once wrote to his friend Boswell "No, Sir, when a man is tired of London, he is tired of life; for there is in London all that life can afford".

**CHARLES DICKENS** (1812–1870): Came to London with his family at the age of eleven. The family fell into debt. Charles was sent to work in a blacking factory, sticking labels on jars. His father was imprisoned for debt. Charles had to fend for himself, living in lodgings in Camden Town. Miserable and hungry, he wandered the London streets. Though the family fortunes soon changed for the better and Charles was able to leave the factory and go to school, it was an experience he never forgot. He eventually became a journalist and writer. Many of his novels first appeared in magazines in serial form. Many contain vivid descriptions of the London that he knew.

# Street names and their origins

**Abingdon Road, W8:** The Abbey of Abingdon was left land here in 1109 by Geoffrey de Vere. The area was subsequently called Abbot's Kensington and the parish church, St. Mary Abbots.

**Aldgate:** Named after one of the four original gates in the City wall leading to the Roman road to Colchester. The Saxon "Aelgate" means open to all, or a free gate.

**Bayswater:** The watering-place belonging to an Anglo-Norman called Bayard and situated where the River Westbourne crossed the Roman Bayswater road. There were several other springs and wells in the gravelly soil of this area.

**Blackfriars:** Named after the great Dominican monastery of the Black Friars which stood here from 1276 until Henry VIII's dissolution of the monasteries in 1538.

**Bloomsbury:** Formerly the bury, or manor house, of William de Blemund who bought the land in 1201. Blemund, or Blémont, means Cornhill which is where the family derived from.

**Bond Street, New and Old, W1:** Named after the speculative builder Sir Thomas Bond of Peckham, who developed the area between 1686 and 1716 where Clarendon House once stood.

**Cannon Street:** Shortened by the cockney dialect from the 12th century original Candelwrichstrete as it was then inhabited by the city's candle-makers and wick chandlers.

**Cheapside:** Derived from the Anglo-Saxon ceap or, "market". It was the City's central market for centuries and was also used for jousts and entertainments.

**Chelsea, SW1:** Originally referred to as "Celchyth", that is a hythe, or landing place, for chalk and lime. The name is also supposed to derive from Chesil, a strand built up by sand and pebbles.

**Clerkenwell:** In the middle ages this was a pleasant village within easy reach of London. The parish clerks of the city would gather once a year at the well, or spring, to put on a biblical play.

**Cornhill:** The City's corn market once stood here on the side of one of the twin hills of London and this is one of the City's earliest recorded names.

**Covent Garden:** Once a garden belonging to Westminster Abbey. It was confiscated by the Crown at the Reformation and sold to the Earl of Bedford in 1552. A market began there in 1661.

**Drury Lane:** Named after Sir Robert Drury, a successful barrister from Suffolk, who bought some land here in about 1500 so that he could build himself a fine town house.

**Ebury Street and Square, SW1:** The 430 acre Eubery farm stood here in Elizabeth I's time. The name is derived from the Saxon "ey", or water, and "burgh," a fortified place.

**Fleet Street:** Originally the Fleet Bridge Road which carried traffic over the River Fleet. This river was named after its "fleot" (Anglo-Saxon for creek or tidal inlet) and rises at the Hampstead and Highgate ponds. Nowadays its course is through underground pipes.

**Goswell Road, EC1:** The original road, like many tracks leading out of the city of London, led to a source of water—Godes' well.

**Harp Lane, EC3:** A "messuage"—a dwelling house with outbuildings and grounds—once stood here. Like many other houses and shops it used a sign to identify itself. In this case, it was the sign of "le harpe".

**Haymarket:** The site, until 1830, of the thrice-weekly market for hay and straw which was established early in the reign of Elizabeth I.

**Holborn:** Named after the "bourne in the hollow" otherwise known as the River Fleet, which is now covered over by Farringdon Street.

**Hyde Park:** Opened to the public by James I, this was originally part of the manor of Ebury, consisting in the 13th century of one hide, i.e. the amount of land which could be tilled in a year by one plough, about 120 acres.

**Johnson's Court, EC4:** Although Dr Samuel Johnson (1709–1784) used to live here between 1765 and 1776, the court was actually named after the Elizabethan antiquarian and merchant tailor, Thomas Johnson.

**Kensington:** Derived from the name of the Saxon village of Chenesitum, or Cynesige's Farm, which grew up near the Roman road—now the High Street.

**Knightrider Street, EC4:** In his 16th century "Survey of London", Stow tells us that this was once part of the way followed by knights as they rode from the Tower Royal at Cannon Street to the jousts and tournaments at Smithfield, or "smooth field" outside the city wall.

**Knightsbridge:** The road from London to Hammersmith followed a bridge over the River Westbourne here. In the 11th century it was called "Cnichtebrugge", the bridge of the serving boy or young man. According to legend, two knights once quarrelled and fought a duel on this bridge.

**Lambeth:** Originally "Lamb's Hythe", the harbour where lambs were loaded or unloaded.

**Leadenhall Market, EC3:** Named after the hall with a leaded roof built by Sir Hugh Nevill in 1309. It was owned by Sir Richard ("Dick") Whittington, Lord Mayor of London, in the early 15th century. After his death it was turned into a granary and poultry market. In 1730 it was rebuilt as a meat market and again rebuilt in 1881.

**Leicester Square, WC2:** The Earl of Leicester built his family mansion on the north side of the square, formerly Leicester fields, between 1635 and 1671 whilst reserving the fields for the traditional use of the local peasants.

**Little Britain, EC1:** The Norman Dukes of Brittany established themselves here in the 13th century, and its original name was Peti Bretane. Until the 18th century it was the centre of the City's book trade, housing many publishers and booksellers. John Milton's "Paradise Lost" was first published here.

**Lombard Street, EC3:** Named after the men from Lombardy in North Italy who took the places of Jewish moneylenders and bankers when the Jews were expelled in the 13th century. The street is still the City's banking centre.

**Mayfair:** Named after the annual fair held during the first two weeks of May at Brook Field on the bank of the River Tyburn. It continued into the early 18th century.

**Millbank, SW1:** The water and wind mills of Westminster Abbey and Palace stood on the riverside during medieval times. The area gradually declined until its redevelopment in the late 19th century.

**Notting Hill Gate:** Called "Knottynghull" in the 14th century the name could derive from the Saxon word "cnott", or hill. It was formerly the site of a turnpike gate where traffic tolls were gathered until 1864.

**Paddington:** The farm or homestead ("ton") of the Paeda family, an early Saxon family who settled in this area.

**Pall Mall, SW1:** In Charles II's time this was a smooth grass alley set aside for the fashionable game of "pale-maille" which the king introduced to England. It was similar in some ways to croquet. Later a new pall mall alley was built in St James's Park which is now the processional avenue, The Mall.

**Petty France, SW1:** At the end of the 15th

century this area was known as "Petefraunce" because it was the home of French wool merchants who came to trade at Westminster. Later, after the Edict of Nantes in 1685, many French refugees settled in this area.

**Piccadilly, W1:** This famous street takes its name from "Pickadel Hall" built by Robert Baker on the old road to Reading. This in turn was named after some of the garments through which this young tailor made his money—the "piccadil", which was a kind of ruff or collar.

**Pimlico:** In Tudor times Ben Pimlico was an innkeeper whose beer was very famous. Then in the early 17th century an inn near Victoria was named after him, and it was from this that the area took its name.

**Portman Square, W1:** Named after Henry William Portman who developed the area in the eighteenth century. He had inherited 270 acres in Marylebone parish which was originally bought in 1553 by Sir William Portman, a West Country knight and Lord Chief Justice of England.

**Portobello Road, W10 & W11:** Originally a cart-track which led to a farm house built by a local farmer called Adams in the early 18th century. He named it Porto Bello Farm after Admiral Vernon captured the town of Porto Bello in the Gulf of Mexico from the Spaniards in 1739. The area was urbanised in the 1860s.

**Printing House Square, EC4:** After the Great Fire of London the King's Printing House was erected here. It was the official printing agency for all royal proclamations, speeches and Acts of Parliament until 1770 when it was moved. Then

in 1785 John Walter founded a paper called *The Daily Universal Register* which changed its name to *The Times* in 1788.

**Pudding Lane, EC4:** The "pudding," or offal, from the butchers' shops in Eastcheap was sent down this lane on its way to the dung boats on the Thames. It was also the starting-point of the Great Fire of London.

**Queensway, W2:** Formerly an old country track called Black Lion Lane after a pub on the corner. One theory is that it was renamed in honour of Queen Victoria, who used to go riding there as a child when she lived at Kensington Palace.

**Regent Street, W1:** Designed by John Nash in the early 19th century for the Prince Regent (later George IV). It was part of a processional way from Carlton House, St James's, to the proposed Regent's Palace in what is now Regent's Park.

**Rolls Passage, EC4:** Documents were once kept in rolls inside pipes housed in the buildings here. Later it became part of the old Public Records Office.

**Saffron Hill, EC1:** One of the finest of the many gardens in medieval London was that of the Bishops of Ely just outside the city wall. It was also an important source of saffron, which was originally grown in East Anglia, and used in the Middle Ages as a dye, a medicine and in cooking.

**St James's, SW1:** In the 11th century a leper asylum dedicated to St James was founded here and run by fourteen chaste maidens. This hospice continued in use until the dissolution of the monasteries in the 16th century, when King

Henry VIII built St James's Palace there and annexed St. James's Park.

**Savoy Place and Street, WC2:** Peter, Count of Savoy, built the Savoy Palace in this area in the mid-13th century. Although he returned to France shortly afterwards many streets and buildings have retained his name.

**Shaftesbury Avenue, W1 and WC2:** A new road opened in 1886 and named after the late 7th Earl of Shaftesbury, a famous 19th century philanthropist. At the end of this road at the centre of Piccadilly Circus stands a monument to Shaftesbury.

**Sloane Street and Square, SW1:** Named after the eminent physician and collector, Hans Sloane, who bought the manor house in Chelsea in 1742 and later died there.

**Soho Square, W1:** Before the square was built in 1681, this was an area of open fields used for hunting. Its name derives from the medieval hunting cry "So-ho"—the English equivalent of the French "tally-ho". This name was also probably given to a local inn popular with huntsmen.

**The Strand, WC2:** In the 12th century this ancient track lay along the river-bank, or "stronde". Since then the land has gradually been reclaimed for building.

**Temple, EC4:** This area was originally the London base of the Knights Templar of Jerusalem, a religious order of knights founded in 1119 who were pledged to protect pilgrims travelling the dangerous roads to the Holy Land. In the 14th century the land was leased to lawyers who were granted the freehold of the Inner and Middle Temple in 1608.

**Threadneedle Street, EC2:** The Merchant Taylors' hall has stood here since the 14th century which may be the origin of the name. In the 18th century the street became the site of the Bank of England, often nicknamed "the old lady of Threadneedle Street".

**Tottenham Court Road, W1:** From before the 12th century this road led from the village of St. Giles-in-the-Fields to the court, or manor house, of Toten Hele which was mentioned in the Domesday Survey of 1086. Toten Hele was probably derived from tote hill, or look-out hill. In the 18th century the manor was demolished to make way for the new road from Paddington, now the Euston Road.

**Tyburn Way, W1:** The site of the famous Tyburn Gallows is commemorated by a plaque on the road-island at Marble Arch. It stood at the junction of the Edgware Road and Tyburn Road (now Oxford Street) so-called because it bridged the river Tyburn ("boundary stream"). The 12 foot high triangular gallows were the site of many celebrated and crowd-pulling executions from the Middle Ages until 1783 when the last hanging took place there.

**Vine Street, W1:** One of several in London called after local vineyards. Vines were widely cultivated in the middle ages.

**Wardrobe Court, off Carter Lane, EC4:** The court marks the site of the house bought in 1359 by Edward III for storing the Royal State Robes. The house was destroyed in the Great Fire of 1666.

**Watling Street, EC4:** Although not an extension of the Roman Dover-Chester road of the same

name, it is possible that both roads derived their names from the same Saxon source. This street was originally called Atheling Street, that is noble or prince's way. This became watheling, and then Watling.

**Westminster:** "The monastery to the west" —named after the monastery which stood there from the 8th century.

# Places to visit

The following abbreviations have been used:
*Ed:* has an education dept.
*H:* provides holiday activities for children.

## ART GALLERIES:

**Courtauld Institute Galleries:** Woburn Square, WC1, 01-580-1015. A general collection of paintings including a superb collection of impressionist and post-impressionist paintings.

**Dulwich College Picture Gallery:** College Road, SE21, 01-693-5254. London's first public art gallery and perhaps one of its most under-rated with some fine paintings by Rembrandt, Gainsborough, Van Dyck and others.

**Guildhall Art Gallery:** King Street, Cheapside, EC2, 01-606-3030. A fascinating collection of pictures of London. Guildhall also incorporates clock museums.

**Hayward Gallery:** South Bank, SE1, 01-928-3144. Houses major art exhibitions organised by the Arts Council. Two open-air sculpture courts.

**National Gallery:** Trafalgar Square, WC2. One of the greatest art collections in the world with examples from the 13th century to 1900. *Ed; H.*

**National Portrait Gallery:** St Martins Place, WC2, 01-930-8511. A comprehensive collection of portraits of the famous from the age of the Tudors to the present day. *Ed; H.*

**Photographer's Gallery:** 8 Great Newport Street, WC1, 01-836-7860. Centre for exhibitions of work by modern and historical photographers. Well stocked photography bookshop.

**Queens' Gallery:** Buckingham Palace, Buckingham Palace Road, SW1, 01-930-4832. A small gallery housing a frequently changing exhibition of items from the Royal Collection.

**Royal Academy of Arts:** Burlington House, Piccadilly, W1, 01-734-9052. Famous for its annual summer exhibition (May to July) which exhibits the work of present day artists. Also houses major loan exhibitions.

**Serpentine Gallery:** Kensington Gardens, W2, 01-402-6075. Set in the middle of the park, this small interesting gallery holds exhibitions of contemporary art.

**Tate Gallery:** Millbank, SW1, 01-828-1212. Important collection of British art. Also general modern art and sculpture. *Ed; H.*

## MUSEUMS:

**Artillery Museum:** The Rotunda, Woolwich Common, SE18, 01-854-2424. Collection of guns and muskets.

**Bear Gardens Museum and Art Centre:** Bear Gardens, Bankside, Southwark, SE1, 01-928-6342. Exhibitions covering 16th and 17th century theatre and the history of Bankside.

**Bethnal Green Museum:** Cambridge Heath Road, E2, 01-980-2415. Fine collection of historic toys, dolls and dolls' houses, costume and model theatres. Also

some 19th century decorative arts. *Ed; H.*

**British Museum:** Great Russell St, London WC1, 01-636-1555. One of the largest and most comprehensive museums in the world. Contains particularly fine collections of Egyptian, Assyrian, Greek, Roman, British, Oriental and Asian antiques. Also fine displays of clocks, manuscripts, stamps and others. *Ed.*

**Geffrye Museum:** Kingsland Road, E2, 01-739-8368. 18th century almshouses with a series of period rooms ranging from 1600 to 1939. *Ed; H.*

**Geological Museum:** Exhibition Road, SW7, 01-589-3444. Exhibitions of gems, minerals, rocks and fossils. Also the "Story of Earth" exhibition which traces the 5,000 million year history of the earth. *Ed.*

**Horniman Museum:** London Road, Forest Hill, SE23, 01-699-2339. Wide-ranging collection of ethnographical and zoological specimens and musical instruments from all over the world. Aquarium. *Ed; H.*

**Imperial War Museum:** Lambeth Road, SE1, 01-735-8922. Exhibits and displays record all aspects of war since 1914. Collections include weapons, equipment, aircraft, armoured vehicles, guns, uniforms, models, paintings and photographs. *Ed.*

**Madam(e) Tussaud's:** Marylebone Road, NW1, 01-935-6861. Life-size wax figures of the famous and infamous, people this fascinating museum. It also includes a Chamber of Horrors and a reconstruction of the *Victory*'s gun-deck during the Battle of Trafalgar.

**Museum of London:** The Barbican, London Wall, EC2, 01-600-3699. A

modern museum illustrating the history of London from prehistoric times to the present day. *Ed; H.*

**Museum of Mankind:** 6 Burlington Gardens, W1, 01-437-2224. A well laid-out series of exhibitions illustrating the life-styles of different tribes and cultures throughout the world.

**National Army Museum:** Royal Hospital Road, SW3. The history of the army from Tudor times to 1914 told through displays of uniforms, weapons, paintings and personal records. *Ed.*

**Natural History Museum:** Cromwell Road, SW7, 01-589-6323. A vast collection of natural history including displays of birds, animals, reptiles and life-size reconstructions of prehistoric monsters. *Ed.*

**National Maritime Museum:** Romney Road, Greenwich, SE10, 01-858-4422. Major collection of Britain's maritime heritage, illustrated by boats, ship models, paintings, navigational instruments and other relics. *Ed; H.*

**Old Royal Observatory:** Greenwich Park, SE10, 01-858-1167. Illustrates the history of the measurement of time, also includes astronomical exhibits.

**Planetarium:** Marylebone Road, NW1, 01-486-1121. Every hour on the hour visitors can see spectacular projections of the night sky and the stars.

**Pollock's Toy Museum:** 1 Scala Street, London, W1, 01-636-3452. A small but fascinating display of old toys, dolls and theatres, including the oldest teddy-bear in England. There is also an

unusual shop.

**Science Museum:** Exhibition Road, SW7, 01-589-6371. History and development of science and industry with a fine collection of working models, engines etc and some fascinating displays. Special children's gallery. *Ed.*

**Tower of London:** Tower Hill, EC3, 01-709-0765. This historic castle houses a wide-ranging collection of armour, historical relics and the Crown Jewels. *Ed.*

**Victoria & Albert Museum:** Cromwell Road, SW7, 01-589-6371. One of the world's outstanding art collections. This vast building houses paintings, sculpture, furniture, tapestries, costumes, ceramics and many other items from all over the world and many different periods. *Ed; H.*

**Wallace Collection:** Hertford House, Manchester Square, W1, 01-935-0687. An important private collection of fine and applied arts from many periods. Particularly noted for its French 18th century paintings, sculpture and furniture.

## GENERAL INTEREST

**All-Hallows-by-the-Tower Church:** Byward Street, EC3. Parts of this church date from AD 675, and it contains an exhibition of Roman and Saxon items, together with a model of Roman London. Also contains a brass-rubbing centre.

**Buckingham Palace:** The Mall, SW1. The Sovereign's principal London home. The Royal Standard is flown when the Queen is in residence. The colourful "Changing of the Guard" usually takes place there every morning.

**Covent Garden:** WC2. Traditionally the site of London's most famous fruit and vegetable market which has now been moved to Nine Elms. The old glass-covered market hall is now being converted into a major transport museum, and the pressure of conservationists has led to the area retaining much of its old atmosphere, with numerous small fashion, craft, speciality shops and interesting restaurants.

**"Cutty Sark" and "Gipsy Moth IV":** Greenwich Pier, SE10. "Cutty Sark" was the last and most famous of the old tea-clippers and is now a beautifully restored museum containing figureheads and maritime relics. "Gipsy Moth IV" nearby was the 53 foot ketch in which Sir Francis Chichester sailed single handed round the world in 1966-67.

**Downing Street:** SW1. The official residences of the Prime Minister and the Chancellor of the Exchequer are at No's 10 and 11 of this street of 17th century houses.

**Hampton Court Palace:** Hampton Court, Middlesex. Cardinal Wolsey built this beautiful palace in 1514 and gave it to Henry VIII. It contains state rooms, a famous picture gallery and its fine gardens contain the infamous "maze".

**Kensington Palace:** Kensington Gardens, W8. Early 17th century royal palace with fine state apartments. Birthplace of Queen Victoria.

**Kenwood House:** Hampstead Lane, NW3. Lying in a 200-acre wooded estate the house contains a fine collection of 18th century paintings and furniture.

**Kew Bridge Engines Museum:** Kew Bridge Road, Middlesex, 01-568-4757. An exhibition of five gigantic steam pumping engines, two of which are in working order. Also a working forge and several traction engines.

**Kew Gardens:** Kew Road, Richmond. The Royal Botanic Gardens is one of the world's greatest collection of trees and plants, with tropical and temperate hot houses, an arboretum, and water gardens in 300 acres. Also in the gardens is the 17th century Kew Palace with its fine collection of bird and animal pictures.

**The Little Angel Marionette Theatre:** 14 Dagmar Passage (off Cross Street), Islington, N1. London's only permanent puppet theatre which performs both modern and traditional fairy-tales and stories usually at week-ends and during school holidays.

**London Dungeon:** 28-34 Tooley Street, SE1. Fascinating new exhibition whose sights and sounds dwell on the horrors of British history.

**London Zoo:** Regent's Park, NW1. One of the most comprehensive zoos in the world, with an open-air aviary, nocturnal houses and an aquarium.

**Monument:** nr. King William Street, EC2. Built to commemorate the Great Fire of London of 1666. There is a magnificent view from the top of its 311 steps.

**Old Bailey:** Newgate Street, EC4. The Central Criminal Court, built on the site of the old Newgate Prison. Trials are open to the public on weekdays.

**Regent's Park Canal:** Extends from Paddington Bridge W2 to Regent's Canal Dock E14. It was built in 1820 to connect Paddington to the Thames, so that goods could be shipped by canal direct to the Port of London from as far away as Birmingham. Canal barge trips are available from Porto'bella Dock on Ladbroke Grove, Little Venice near Warwick Avenue and Camden Lock on Chalk Farm Road.

**Royal Mews:** Buckingham Palace Road, SW1. Royal carriages, horses and equipage. Open on Wednesday and Thursday afternoons, except in Ascot week in June.

**St. Katherine-by-the-Tower:** St. Katherine's Way, E1. A large leisure complex situated on the old St. Katherine's Dock which includes a yacht haven and a floating maritime museum. The Maritime Trust have now moved several of their historic craft here from different parts of Britain including the steam herring drifter "Lydia Eva", the Thames sailing barge "Cambria" and the West Country trading schooner "Kathleen and May".

**St. Paul's Cathedral:** Ludgate Hill, EC4. This magnificent domed building was built in 1675-1710 by Sir Christopher Wren to replace a previous church that had been destroyed in the Great Fire.

**Speakers' Corner:** nr. Marble Arch, Hyde Park, W1. Traditional venue for the soap-box orators who address anyone willing to listen on a variety of topics—frequently religion and politics. Best on Sunday all-day, and Saturday evening.

**Stock Exchange:** Old Broad Street, EC2. The visitors' gallery overlooks about 4,000 members milling around on the Trading Floor. There are guided talks and film shows.

**Syon Park and House:** Park Road, Isleworth, Middlesex. The 55 acres surrounding this 16th century mansion also contain a garden centre.

**Trafalgar Square:** W1. This spacious, pleasant square was laid out in 1829 to commemorate Nelson's victory at Trafalgar. Dominated by Nelson's 182 ft. high column. Famous for its New Year's Eve festivities.

**Westminster: Big Ben and the Houses of Parliament:** Parliament Square, SW1. Debates in the House of Commons can be heard from the Stranger's Gallery on some weekday afternoons from mid-October to July. On other days there is a special tour of Parliament at appointed times.

**Westminster Abbey:** Parliament Square, SW1. The original 11th century abbey has been altered and enlarged at many times in its colourful history. Interesting aspects include the mediaeval Coronation Chair, Poets' Corner and the Brass-Rubbing Centre.

**Westminster Cathedral:** Ashley Place, SW1. Largest and most important Roman Catholic Church in England with some mosaics, and fine views from the tower.

## MARKETS

**Camden Passage:** Islington High Street, N1. A network of tiny antique shops along paved streets. It is particularly busy and lined with antique and bric-a-brac stalls on Wednesdays and Saturdays.

**Dingwall's Market:** Camden Lock, Camden High Street, NW1. A small, friendly weekend market of stalls selling everything from good quality second-hand clothes to crafts and antiques.

**New Caledonian:** Tower Bridge Road, SE1. Known as the dealer's antique market and held on Fridays. As with other antique markets, it must be visited early to get real bargains.

**Petticoat Lane:** Middlesex Street, E1. A huge, rambling market held on Sunday mornings. Stalls sell everything from modern tat to antiques. Some streets specialise such as Brick Lane (furniture and electrical equipment) and Club Row (fish, birds, reptiles, and mammals).

**Portobello Road:** W11. A fruit and vegetable market during the week, on Saturday the market extends from the antique stalls at the Notting Hill Gate end through the fruit and vegetable market to the clothes and bric-a-brac of the north end. Lively, bustling atmosphere.

## INFORMATION CENTRES:

**British Tourist Authority:** 01-629-9191, 64 St James's Street, SW1. Enquiry centre on tourism in Britain with a wide range of tourist literature both free and for sale.

**City of London Information Centre:** 01-606-3030, St. Paul's Churchyard, EC4. Information and advice mostly about the City.

**London Tourist Board:** 4 Grosvenor Gardens, SW1, 01-730-0791/3400. Provides advice and literature on events, places-to-visit, and accommodation in London.

**Recorded information:** Children's London: 01-246-8007
Teletourist: 01-246-8041

# Books to read

There are a large number of books available about London. These range from historical surveys of different areas of London to books on architecture, geography, parks, wild life, language, entertainments and customs and ceremonies. If you live in London your local library will have a specialist collection of books relating to your area. The following list is a very brief guide to books of general interest, many of them in paperback. The Museum of London sells a large range of books on London. Its own booklets on various periods of London history are very informative and relatively inexpensive.

## GUIDE BOOKS

**Penguin guide to London** by F. R. Banks (Penguin 1978). General guide with maps and plans.

**The companion guide to London** by D. Piper (Fontana 1974). Excellent general guide with a large section on the City.

**The Blue Guide to London** by S. Rossiter (Benn 1978). Illustrated guide with maps.

**Help yourself in London** by Michael Balfour (Garnstone Press 1970). A guide to services, facilities and things to do.

**Parents' Guide to Children's London** by F. Morgan & L. Newnham Roberts (Nicholson Publications).

**Kids' Historic London** by Elizabeth Holt and Molly Perham (Abelard-Schuman 1976). Comprehensive guide to places to visit and things to do for children in London.

**London: Your sightseeing guide** (British Tourist Authority). Very useful annual tourist guide.

**Village London** by the *Observer* Magazine staff. (Arrow 1978). Area by area guide to shops, and restaurants and places of interest.

**London for the disabled** by Freda Bruce Lockhart (Ward Lock 1971). Complete guide to facilities for the disabled in London.

**On Location: London** by Jeanne Streatfield (Mills and Boon 1976). A book for children exploring London.

**Young Visitor's Guide to the City of London** by Jean Davis (Published by the Guildhall). A short, well illustrated guide.

**Daily Telegraph Children's Guide to London** by Caroline Brakespear and Helen Mann (Collins 1979). By two London mothers who write from experience.

## SPECIALIST GUIDES

**Pocket Guide to Dickens' London** by Geoffrey Fletcher. (*Daily Telegraph* 1969). One of a series of books by the same author on the different aspects of London, highlighting the off-beat and eccentric.

**London Street Names** by Gillian Bebbington (Batsford 1972). Brief but fascinating guide to the origins of street names.

**Where the Famous Lived in London** by Christopher Mann (Serpentine Press 1974). Illustrated guide to the houses where 30 of London's most interesting residents or visitors once lived.

## GENERAL HISTORY

**London: 2000 years of a city and its people** by F. Barker and P. Jackson (Cassell 1974). Illustrated, and detailed account of London's history.

**London: The biography of a city** by Christopher Hibbert (Longmans 1969).

**London: a concise history** by Geoffrey Trease (Thames and Hudson 1975). Very readable account of London life from Roman times to the present day.

**London: a Pictorial History** by John Hayes (Batsford 1972). A beautifully illustrated and concise general history.

**London's Guilds and Liveries** by John Kennedy Melling (Shire Publications 1972).

**London Bridge** by Peter Jackson (Cassell 1972). A fascinating history.

---

# Acknowledgments

**Photographs**
Key to position of photographs: (T) top; (B) bottom; (C) centre; (R) right; (L) left.

Aerofilms: 31(TR); Peter Baistow: 41(CR); Bank of England: 29(B); Barnaby's Picture Library: 41(TR); British Library: 14–15, 15(T), 16–17, 42(L); British Museum/John Freeman: 19(T), 20–21, 27(BR), 30, 34(T&B), 44(B), 49(T); British Museum/Michael Holford: 28(L); British Tourist Authority: 31(BR); Camera Press: 46(R); Cooper Bridgeman: 32(C); Eric Crichton: 52(C); Daily Telegraph Colour Library/ Judith Aronson: 51(CL); Hallman: 9(TL), 51(TR); Tim Mercer: 45(TR); Homer Sykes: 9(C); Patrick Ward: 29(TR); Adam Woolfit: 42(R), 43(TR); Robert Estall: 8(TL); Mary Evans Picture Library: 15(B); Sally Fear: 40(C), 41(TL); Fotomas Index: 36(CR); Fox Photos: 39(T), 43(B); Michael Freeman: 10(TR), 11(TL), 14(B), 28(BR), 47(TR), 48(TR), front endpapers, contents; Richard and Sally Greenhill: 21(BL); Guildhall Library: 15(C), 33(B); John Hillelson Agency/Bruno Barbey/Magnum Photos: 45(TL); Neil Holmes: 36(CL); Angelo Hornak: 11(B), 24(TL); Illustrated London News: 33(C), 35(B); London Transport Executive: 50(L), 53(TL); Macdonald Educational: 35(TL); Mansell Collection: 23(C), 31(CL), 37(CL), 43(TL), 48(BL); Margaret Murray: 41(C); Museum of London: 12, 13(T&B), 21(TR), (BC), (BR), 18(BR), 22–23, 23(T), 24(BR), 25(T), (C), (BL), (BR), 26(T), (BL), (BR), 27(L), 32(BL), (BR), 33(T), 35(TR), 37(T), (B), 43(C); Mike Peters: 10(B), 11(TR), (C), 29(TL), 47(BR), 51(BL); Port of London Authority: 31(CR); Portal Gallery/John Allin: 40(B); Press Association: 45(B); Radio Times Hulton Picture Library: 31(TL), (BL), 37(CR), 38(T), (BL), (CB), (BR), 39(BL), (CB), (BR), 52(BL); Rex Features: 47(BL), 51(TL), (BR); Royal Borough of Kensington and Chelsea Local History Collection: 53(TR); Royal Society: 24(BL); By courtesy of the Marquess of Salisbury: 18(T); Savoy Hotels Ltd/Peter Myers: 48(TL); John Sims: 14(C), 48(BR), 49(C), (CR), (BR), contents; Shaun Skelly: 9(TR), 10(TL), 53(B); Society of Antiquaries: 44(T); Spectrum Colour Library: 8(B), 40(CL), 52(BR); Homer Sykes: 8(C), 9(BR), 49(BL), 50(R), endpapers; John Watney: 46(L), 47(TL); Reg Wilson: 19(B).

**Artists**
Jon Blake
Chris Forsey
Hayward Art Group
Tony Payne

# Index